Enlighten Up!

Practical Wisdom &
Spiritual Guidance for
an Imperfect World

Cathy Langlois

Enlighten-Up!
Practical Wisdom and Spiritual Guidance for an Imperfect World

Cathy Langlois

Published by Spirit Horse Productions

ISBN 978-0-9986125-0-8

Praise for Enlighten-Up!

"It's very refreshing to encounter a clear recital of helpful information and practice that is not all gussied up in the gift wrapping of another culture and will complement any spiritual practice. Cathy Langlois' deceptively simple book, written in the most ordinary English, is a bright beam from a kind and very open heart. These lovely pages are the utterances of a 'settled,' wide-awake woman, someone you should know if you don't. This book will be a big hug of useful information. I was charmed."

Peter Coyote, actor/writer/ordained Zen Buddhist Priest.

"Enlighten-Up! is filled with easy-to-understand yet profoundly important steps for all of us to live up to our potential as full human beings. This book has echoes of the endless wisdom from the great Maya Angelou: how we must learn from our defeats and not be discouraged, and how, if we practice a higher level of civility and inclusiveness, we also elevate ourselves. This book also confronts our natural fear of change and of people not like ourselves and helps guide us through these irrational feelings. It is a brave and practical book that, for the open-minded, can have a long-lasting and deeply meaningful impact on our lives."

Bob Hercules, Co-Director, "Maya Angelou: And Still I Rise"

"This is a humorous, remarkably well-written, and spiritually spot-on book. I found myself laughing out loud, shaking my head in wonder, and sometimes tears would visit my eyes. It touched my soul."

Dr. Thomas Cushing, PhD, JD

"Enlighten-Up! is packed with spiritual wisdom, teachings, and guidance and is written in a style everyone can understand and enjoy. Read a chapter or two when you need a lift, a kick in the pants, tidbits of wisdom, are searching for an answer, or all of the above. A must-have book for any spiritual seeker.

Rebecca Germolus, marketing consultant and blogger

"Cathy Langlois has the rare gift of clarity and wisdom to help you identify what is really behind a problem and then guide you to the right answers. Whether you would like more joy in your life on a daily basis or need to make significant changes, this is a book you will return to over and over again."

Howard VanEs, President, Let's Write Books, Inc.

"Such a refreshing read ... obviously written by one who has walked the walk and is now sharing her experience with clarity and candor. It has the properties of an inner mirror, yet manages to deliver the stark truth with a tender and wise spirit."

René Jenkins, ceremonial sound practitioner and healing performance artist

"*Enlighten Up!* is an insightful, engaging group of stories designed to help you crack open your perspective, alternately shining the light upon you or stoking the fire of your own light to burst forth. Thank you, Cathy, for the humor and compassion you bring to encouraging us all to find our way."

Sondra Beam, herbal pharmacy manager and student

Acknowledgements

*A*most important thank-you and love to my generous and patient husband, Bob Wolcott, who helps me find humor when it seems none is available. He is truly among the best of men and his support and encouragement made this book possible. I send deep gratitude to my best friend and cheerleader, Natasha Lynn, whose optimism, talent, healing, and listening skills are a gift to behold. Thanks to fellow survivor, my brother Bill Langlois, for your indefatigable spirit and our many profound conversations.

Thank you to the multi-talented Peter Coyote, whose fearless and beautiful writing in his recent book, The *Rainman's Third Cure*, inspired me to be unafraid to put my soul on the page.

Many thanks to Dr. Tom Cushing for his support, wise counsel, and enthusiasm as a beta reader and Rebecca Germolus, whose generous insights, feedback, and input helped get me through the learning process of my first book.

I want to express my great appreciation for Howard VanEs and his expert team at Let's Write Books, Inc., for the support, communication, and invaluable contribution in putting this book together and getting it out into the world. Also thanks to the talented artists Molly Fisher (for the beautiful cover art) and Dana Vallarino (for whimsical chapter symbols).

I will always be grateful to every teacher, student, client, and friend who has crossed my path in this life. I learned from all of you and you are reflected in these pages in many ways. But a special acknowledgement needs to go to all the students at Spirit Horse for your spiritual insight, enthusiasm, and the generosity you show in sharing your stories. It's my honor to assist you on your path.

Love to all my critters here and gone ... teachers every one.

Table of Contents

INNER VOICE

CREATIVITY

Introduction

I didn't have a single friend or even acquaintance in the new town I'd arrived in. I had no job or place to live and very limited finances, alternately sleeping in my car or living in a campground. At the time, I thought I was on a magical-mystery camping adventure; now I suppose you'd call it being homeless. I was running away from heartbreak, my dysfunctional family, and a dead-end career.

Rolling in from the road after three months of cross-country travel, I landed on the West Coast with everything I owned jammed into an orange VW Bug. I was road weary, lonely, and more confused than I'd been when I'd started my "intuitive travels" to seek my path in the world. And then a simple question changed the course of my future.

As I wandered through town, I found my first necessity: a good coffee shop. Nursing my second refill and watching the world pass by the window, I spotted a hair salon called Good Karma across the street and decided to splurge on a haircut, trusting it would be a good one based on the name.

As I entertained the hairdresser with a story about an accidental meeting with this cool monk guy who'd blessed my travels (it was the Dalai Lama, whose identity was unknown to me at the time), I noticed a slight, elderly woman in the next chair eavesdropping with great interest. She leaned toward me with kind, sparkling eyes and asked, "My dear, what is it you're looking for?"

To my great embarrassment, I fumbled for words to answer her and started crying. The pain I was running from, the loneliness from days of isolated searching, poured out into the willing ears of this compassionate stranger. I don't think I'd even really asked myself that question. If I had, you can bet the fear and pain I was trying to escape from distracted me from the answer.

There's such power in a question. Why are you here? What do you want? What are you looking for? Big answers are revealed in quiet moments.

When the emotion subsided, she suggested I get a healing at a meditation center she attended. Taking that step started me on the next leg of a journey I've been traveling my whole life: seeking peace through communication and understanding about our purpose in this world.

After all was said and done, my explorations of various spiritual wisdom traditions all led to the same place—all forms of healing, meditation, prayer and teaching have the ability transform your life ... if you're ready. They ultimately guide you to discover the truth and insight within you. That's where your answers are anyway; that's where you'll find your peace.

Everyone endures times of despair from broken relationships, unexpected loss, emotional blows, or the struggle to find meaning and direction in life. Wrestling with unnamed pain and depression is too often treated with medication instead of spiritual guidance on how to heal it from within. We've all been there and will be again; such is the nature of life and growth. You can pretty much count on uncontrolled shifts of reality to challenge us on our path.

But here's one thing I know for sure: help is everywhere. A bit of overheard conversation, kindness from a stranger, or a random passage in a book can be the well-placed truth or question that moves you from stuck to unstuck. I wrote this book from the questions, phrases, and insights that helped light the way for me so that I could share the realizations they were born from.

So, if you're lonely, feeling stuck and indecisive, unable to change or make a decision, or just need a catalyst for your day, pick up this book and read whatever chapter it opens to. It most likely will be exactly what you need! I hope some of the insight I've gained though my journey can help you get on down the road and find some light there.

Bonus for Readers of Enlighten-Up!

Get a FREE audio download from Cathy Langlois featuring simple techniques to help you find your balance, regain focus, increase your enthusiasm for the world around you, and live a more centered life. The audio includes three parts:

Grounding & Releasing: You'll feel more present by connecting your spirit and body to the earth. You can then easily let go of problems that block your natural flow of energy and restore a sense of peace.

Re-owning Life Force: (Chi) This is a powerful but simple way to replenish your life force and call back all the energy you've been giving away (problems, people, projects etc.).

Protection: A visualization to help you create a safety zone from negative people and events.

**Download your FREE audio at
www.SpiritHorseCenter.com/bonus**

Communication

Be Receptive to New Information, but Always Look at Things for Yourself

o you consider yourself open-minded?

Curiosity and questions open you to new awareness about things as simple as making the perfect risotto or as profound as the nature of the Universe. Either way, an open mind is imperative for learning and expanding your field of knowledge and consciousness. You can discover a lot by taking notice of those around you. When you're in a receptive state, communication between you and others flows with a natural give and take. This is a valuable tool for developing compassionate listening and increased understanding of ourselves and others.

So, by all means, listen without judgement, question with genuine curiosity, and see what you uncover. But when knowledge is examined in the light of your own truth, you may find that some of the info needs to be discarded. We often jettison things because they're threatening or uncomfortable, but the new input could actually be pointing out that a belief no longer serves you and is in fact false!

There's no need to make yourself or anyone else right or wrong when coming up with answers; feel free to walk away if someone tries to use undue influence and force their truth on you. There's as many different paths and solutions as people. Hopefully our individual life experiences teach us what we most need to learn.

Don't despair when you find yourself in the middle of a seemingly unsolvable problem. You never know how many attempts it took your soul to create the exact situation you're having for the growth you need. It may be from this life or even a past life. Be open to the answers you may find in them. Your spirit knows best and brings you what you need.

It's also helpful to hold those who share their knowledge with you in high regard. Somebody else's life view is valuable even if you don't agree with it. Who knows, down the road it may suddenly become relevant. As Shakespeare said, "There are more things in heaven and earth Horatio, than are dreamt of in your philosophy." Expanding your mind means considering possibilities that are not your current reality.

Stay receptive and you never know what will show up. It's that unexpected turn in the road you didn't know you asked for that leads you to miracles. If you aren't paying attention, no worries. It'll find you again in a different form. I had a wonderful student who, when examining some unexpected turn on her path, would declare, "Nothing's by coincidence!"

Openness check: Did you learn anything new today? In conversation, do you really listen or just wait until someone stops speaking to give an already prepared opinion? Can you see things from a different perspective than your own? What is that like when you do?

Question, explore, listen, review.

When in Doubt Ask, Does This Bring Grace into My Life?

y thesaurus says grace is a pleasant way of behaving: a charming, attractive trait, divine assistance, or an act of kindness or courtesy. How do you move through your life?

While racing around on errands, bombarded by rudeness and inconsideration from others, do you feel angry and less kind? How do you respond to it? At the bank, a harried mother didn't thank me for opening a door for her and I snippily thought, "Well I won't do that again." How spiritual of me!

How often do you let a car cut in front of you in traffic without swearing at them? Do you regularly smile at strangers for no reason?

If the activities of your everyday life are making you irritable and inconsiderate, make a list of what causes the most stress and diminishes your soul. Upon inspection, you might find that it's time to make some changes.

It's easy to get drawn into negative gossip, complaining and needlessly judging ourselves and others. But each time you do, it radiates a lack of grace and your soul contracts, pulling you away from life and drawing the same energy back to you. Unhappy, harsh energy tends to feed on itself, robbing you of the peaceful, contented feeling grace affords us in this imperfect world. Making a decision to live life with more gentleness and understanding is a good start in setting the tone of what you wish to experience every day.

You have the right to say no to anything that doesn't support and bring out the best in you and others. Changing your life can be as easy as just choosing to be a person who wishes to contribute more grace into the world and supporting others who do too.

Kindness rules!

If you're considering an activity you're in doubt about, it might be as basic as asking if it makes you feel good about yourself. Taking time to notice the situations and people that contribute to a negative or positive outlook might be all you need.

If You Give What Can't Be Received, There's Going to Be Trouble

*O*uch! You lay gasping in disbelief, kicked in the gut by an unexpected betrayal or rejection. How could it be? You diligently listened to their endless problems. You doled out your best advice, did countless favors, gave healing and comfort to their families, friends, dogs, cats—you name it. What did you do wrong; how can you fix it?

There are always people whose damage requires them to be takers. If they don't feel worthy or lovable—or worse, if they enjoy the drama of unfixable problems—there's little you can do to solve it. They'll deplete your energy and when you don't disconnect, leave you feeling like you've somehow failed them. It's a hard truth and one that puts healers and fixers in a huge dilemma. After all, communication heals all things, right? Not if the person is deaf and blind to the truth it doesn't.

I experienced this with a long-time friend I'd often supported and counseled about her many volatile encounters with those in her life. In our last conversation, I pointed out that she was often attracted to the type of person she knew was going to eventually abuse her. I suggested she step back and take a clear look next time before jumping into the relationship. That did it! I was now the abuser in her mind. She put me in the role she needed me to be in to reject the truth I offered. I told her something she was not ready to hear and trouble did indeed follow.

There was no amount of giving or healing that was going to fix this relationship now that I'd let the genie out of the bottle. The gift for me was in learning to take a step back, examine my pattern of picking friends unable to receive what I offered, and ask myself why I sought validation by trying to save them.

In that situation, you'll actually become less respected and valuable to them the more you give. This is akin to the old adage ... who wants to belong to a club that would have you as a member? If (God forbid) you start changing and feel less of a need to heal them, you'll be out the door anyway. A taker needs an out-of-control giver to survive and they're very skilled at finding them, so consider it a sign of spiritual health if they've left your life, even if in a nasty way.

It's important to remember that we can all be takers at times and not be ready to hear truths we might need. If the overall communication is good but you 've hit a bump in the road, hang in there, leave them alone, and trust that you will be able to communicate in the future. Some things are too painful to hear and have to dawn gradually as you're ready to face them.

There are always signs pointing to a person's true character if you're paying attention. You can dodge the bullet if you take the time to examine these disturbing relationships. Sometimes this helps you determine if you should duck or if it's a valuable enough connection to hang in there for.

Your own needs and damage can blind you to what's truly going on and the game you signed on for. But in retrospect, it's not usually a surprise, is it? You couldn't hear or see through that brick wall you were running toward. Be careful not to give it all away to someone who isn't prepared to receive and maybe ask yourself why you feel the need to do that in the first place. Apply your new-found wisdom to create healthier relationships and move on.

If you're in doubt about a relationship that's bugging you check out how they act toward others (I always pay attention to how people treat waiters and waitresses). What do they say about other people? Are you drained after spending time with them? Is your friendship healthy enough to weather this temporary difficulty or is it a pattern?

We're in it Together, but Empathy Doesn't Mean Taking on the Pain and Problems of Others

I always feel better when someone listens to me, especially if I'm indulging in a good old pity party about the misadventures of my life. I don't really want them to solve my problems or sympathize. I mostly just need the validation that comes when someone else bears witness to the mess I am experiencing and my feelings about it.

Listening is an art that's fueled by empathy: the basic ability to understand the perspective and emotions of another. This is an ability of the second chakra (emotion, intimacy, connection).

When empathy gets out of control, however, you can take on emotions and illnesses from other people. Have you found yourself irritated and cranky after the ranting of a frustrated and angry spouse, family member, or co-worker? Have you experienced a drop in energy after a conversation with a down-and-out friend? This frequently happens when you're pulled into solving the issue and take on the energy and emotion of the situation.

Can you give advice when you're having empathy for someone? The question really is, should you? Advice is an attempt to fix something. You're no longer the neutral listener and have assumed some responsibility for the problem. Worse, it'll be all your fault if your advice doesn't work. When someone's unleashing a torrent of troubles, they're not ready for solutions anyway.

Your best bet is to stay uninvolved (neutral) and be a sounding board for whatever action they feel they need to take, unless they're planning something criminal or self-destructive, in which case, feel free to go all parental on them!

Self-preservation is a necessity for empaths and entails clear boundaries about what you can give without damaging yourself. If you have a confirmed drama queen in your life who relishes spewing out energy and emotion, protect yourself by being grounded and aware before you interact. You may need to have more empathy for yourself than for them and take steps to be less accessible.

We Often Try to Fix in Others What We Need to Heal in Ourselves

*O*nce upon a time, Princess Charisma believed power had been divinely bequeathed to her to fix the poor, clueless souls she came across in her life. She lectured with great beneficence to all in hearing range, freely sharing theories most politically correct, exposing erroneous beliefs, and urging all to admit their shortcomings and amend their ways.

Dissenters were subject to longer rants about what would improve their meager lives, until they finally agreed with her. She expounded loudly about her dedication to absolute honesty even while bragging about her talent to manipulate others to do her bidding.

Priding herself on her ability to listen, she heard not a word, unless to extol her virtues. Claiming to cherish communication, she cast aside anyone who spoke words unsupportive of her version of reality. "I'm only coming from love!" was her mantra, yet she seemed ignorant to the simplest needs of those around her.

One day a ginger-haired child stood up from the hypnotized crowd sitting at her feet and quietly said, "Princess, can I give you a gift, please?"

With a pleased smile the princess pompously nodded at the child, who clumsily placed in her hands a package wrapped in a filthy, burlap bag. The little girl bowed and backed up into the crowd.

Flinging the bag to the ground, she pulled out a metal oval covered in beautiful swirls of color. It glowed with tranquil blue and royal purple and a piney odor from the verdant green drifted on the gentle wind. Warmth radiated from the glowing, golden yellow and the swaths of orange and red sizzled. It was a living, vibrant picture of life.

She held it up to the crowd admiring it with delight declaring, "This is the most beautiful of gifts I could have received. Look at this symbol of my wisdom that could also be yours!" She moved the circle from side to side so all could marvel at the wonderful present bestowed upon her.

The crowd grew silent, glancing at each other and shaking their heads as if waking from a dream. Several people stood and turned to walk away. Confused, the princess cried, "Behold the symbol of my truth!" Many more started mumbling, heading off on the path to town and home.

"Why are you going? I have so much more to teach you!" She felt a tug on the hem of her dress and looked down to see the quizzical look of the little gift giver.

"You're looking at the wrong side; the other side is the gift!"

The princess turned over the disc, blinded for a moment by the reflected sun and at last saw only the frowning image of her own face.

Have you been or do you know a princess like this one? If you spend an abundance of time and energy fixing or judging other people's issues, it might be time to take a look in the mirror. Sometimes the desire to fix others stems from a need to distance yourself from the discomfort their problems are stimulating. What is the situation reflecting in your own life?

Fairy tales were often used as metaphors to impart lessons and I've borrowed liberally from them here—particularly the revelation of truth by an innocent from "The Emperor's New Clothes."

Don't be a Dumpster– Communication is Two Way; Dumping is One

*A*nybody in your life you avoid conversations with? You know, that friend who gets you on the phone and never takes a breath. You set down the phone, go brush your teeth, come back, pick it up gurgling, "Uh huh," and they don't even notice. Side effects of being dumped on can include headache, stomach pain, feeling drained, and an unreasonable urge to take a shower!

There are times we desperately want to be listened to more than we need to exchange conversation and that's normal. But what happens when you get so stuck in your pain and need that the only relief is to dump it on someone else so you feel better?

This is not two-way communication and if you are in the role of listener, your feedback is rarely heard. You'll be pulled into a litany of unsolvable problems with your solutions cast aside by excuses and rationalizations. This is not a conversation for healing and connection.

This is a release of unwanted, unowned emotions and problems for the person dumping.

It's a very unfulfilling communication when two people aren't truly hearing each other and responding from a place of real connection and understanding. The loser here will be the person getting dumped on. If this happen often, you may need to ask yourself what you get from playing a martyred listener to a perpetual victim. It takes two to play this game, so if it's a habit, you play a part as well.

My favorite dumper was the one who ranted on about shoddy treatment by family and friends who didn't pay attention to her. It never registered that I was, in fact, listening to her. My responses and sympathies went unheard and after a recital of injustices and insurmountable problems, she immediately called another friend to run the exact same program.

The answers we seek are often found by being attentive to someone else's life story and sharing mutual experiences and truth. Honest two-way communication can reveal you to yourself, deepen your relationships, and introduce new ways of viewing your life. So, listen already!

Do you need to vent your emotions right away so you feel better? After conversations, can you remember what was said or what was going on for the other person? Are people starting to avoid you? Do you feel like you are on the receiving end of a lot of other people's woes?

If You Need Validation,
Seeking it Will Control You

*W*e've all had twenty-twenty hindsight about bad choices made based on someone else's information. Do you ask everybody's advice when you're making a decision? Can you trust your own truth or do you second guess everything you think? When you place your value on the opinion of others you lose the power to be autonomous and be your authentic self.

Low self-esteem from a tough childhood, past life damage, insecurity about previous poor choices, normal self-doubt from a lack of information, or not being present in your body (for a variety of reasons) can all cause self-doubt. Unfortunately, these are all pretty typical experiences we encounter as we grow, change, and learn.

Not moving out of that spot, however, is what makes seeking external validation a crippling pattern. While it may be good to gather information from those we trust or from an expert in the area we seek answers in, trouble arises when we give external information, advice, and opinions more power than our own truth. This is how you give away your seniority to something or someone outside yourself.

Seniority is a state of confidence in your ability to choose, respond, and recover in any given situation. This includes having the discernment to weigh all information and apply your own knowledge to the situation. This is a natural ability of the seventh, or crown, chakra (connection to higher spirit to give you a bigger picture of life). Seniority is not dependent on whether or not someone else agrees with or approves of us.

Getting stuck on external validation leads to making decisions based on things that might not be true for you at all. The more you do this, the more it contributes to a loss of personal power. In effect, you're lying to yourself and accepting something not right for you in order to be liked. After all, there will always be those who don't approve of your choices. You can drive yourself crazy trying to get everybody's approval about your actions.

Confusion and indecisiveness are pretty prevalent if you're caught in this pattern. There's really no perfect image, behavior, or success you need acquire to simply own the answers you get from the beautiful soul you are. Wouldn't it be great if it was mandatory in our schools to teach classes on how to trust and listen to ourselves? *Meditation 101.*

Slow down, find a moment to sit in a quiet space and ask yourself what you really want to do and what you really believe. Don't worry about anybody else's response to your choice. Whose opinion is more important than yours?

Is There a Conversation Between Your Spirit and Your Body? Anybody Listening?

*I*magine for a moment that you're a spirit inhabiting a human body of your own design. Genetics, self-care, environment, and a variety of outside influences can affect that physical self. But you picked it and made a choice to be here on this planet at this time. Love it or not, this is the body you chose. What are you doing with it? Is there a partnership between you (the spirit) and your body? Are you present in it well enough so it serves your spiritual purpose for being here?

The emphasis on perfection in physical appearance and performance can start to deaden you to the soul's reason for having a body to begin with. Particularly if self judgement of your imperfections has you jumping on the never-ending treadmill of spending so much time improving yourself that you have no time left to enjoy life. Who is making this determination of perfection for you anyway?

We give up a lot of power to the physical, spending an inordinate amount of time stashing money in the body bank—and not enough in day-to-day activities that feed the soul. I hate to point out the obvious, but guess which one continues on after this life ends?

When body and spirit are in communication, your body becomes a much happier home for the soul. Who's running the show? When your body is, you mostly hear what it needs in order to survive and your time gets spent pursuing only physical well-being. Put your spirit back in the driver's seat and the body will relax, feeling safer and trusting that someone is in charge who has unconditional love for it. It's often easier to give that unconditional love to the people we care about and forget to give it to our own body, mind, and spirit. When your spirit takes charge, you'll not only make the body happier, but raise the energy vibration so more of your life force can be utilized through it. Everybody loves having more energy!

Listen ... what does your body want so you can thrive and can enjoy being in it? Have a conversation with your body as if you're calling a friend. Tell it you love it no matter what and ask, "What do you need to be well and safe today?" Bodies give you simple answers like sleep, water, exercise, greens, or sex. Do your best to provide what's asked for and it'll be easier to be present and comfortable so your spirit shines brighter through it. Eventually you'll start aligning your path with who you are on the inside and life will become a more fulfilling experience.

Good Rationalizing Means Lots of Practice Lying to Yourself

I sat patiently in my chair, eyes glazed over, listening to a well-rehearsed lie about the noble intentions in a student's cruel act. Nodding politely, I silently waited for her to finish. This spurred her on to an even longer explanation of the logic and reasoning behind said action. It all made sense to her. I'm sure she spent a huge amount of time analyzing this justification and she used many casual inflections and shrugs to underline it wasn't a big deal.

When she finally finished, I quietly said, "Well, thanks for your explanation, but I don't think you're telling me the truth." This set her off in another long-winded tirade about why it was true and here's why I should believe her.

Generally, I've learned that the more words someone throws at me when supposedly telling the truth, the less true it actually is. This doesn't necessarily mean they're consciously lying. It may just be too painful for them to own up to the actual truth. Saving face, or avoidance of an unpleasant reality, is strong motivation for lying.

Therein lies the self-preservation technique we call rationalization. A much-overused tool of that big old brain of ours. It's a convoluted story we tell ourselves (and others) to justify our inability to face our accountability for something.

If you really listen to people, they get nervous if they're lying to you and/or themselves. Many excuses get thrown into the mix with an excess of words and reasons for the situation. They might even throw someone else under the bus to prop up their side or contradict a previous statement. Whatever works to keep up the illusion. Sometimes, we all need rationalizations to help us get through the night until we have enough courage to let them go.

It may require an act of kindness at times to feign ignorance, let them have their cover, and hope they can eventually face the truth. In other situations, you might be called on to hold the line, clearly, neutrally state what you see, and move on from that conversation. Should you find yourself trying to convince them with too many of your words, you might be doing the same thing they are!

The next time you're concocting a long story about some event in your life, ask yourself what the main emotion is you're feeling. What is it you don't really want to own up to?

Persist in Speaking Your Truth—You'll Piss Some People Off, but Do It Anyway

*Y*ou can try to please everybody and say the right thing, but at some point, it's still not going to be what they want to hear and somebody's going to get mad. What a lot of work it is to monitor what you truly want to say, altering it constantly to fit the current sensibility of the room. While the political correctness movement is an invaluable guide to increase awareness and education on the use of offensive words and thoughts, it's often now misused and applied to those who disagree with us. I see people hesitant to express a difference of opinion because they're afraid of being labeled "politically incorrect."

What do you really think and feel, and why are you making the decisions you are? Craving acceptance, we can withhold our speech, feeling unworthy to be heard and ultimately lose contact with our authentic self. If you only speak words that cause the least conflict or reaction, there's no stimulation for exchanging new ideas or philosophies. How do you grow if there are no differences?

Now, we don't need to run around blathering our opinions and judgements to everyone we meet and there's certainly a time to use temperance to avoid needless injury. But when did it become the norm not to communicate and tell each other the truth or to shout someone down until they agree with us?

If I have a big, emotional reaction to a comment, either related to me or someone else, I know there's something there I need to explore. This usually means it's time for a heart-to-heart discussion or some self-introspection to get to the truth of the matter and restore harmony and connection.

But if you're dealing with someone who's being judgmental or a basic jerk with intent to hurt, blow them off! It's a sign of self-preservation to have strong emotion in the face of cruelty. Who wants to listen to destructive criticism?

However, honest communication that offers a different perspective on behavior, attitudes. or beliefs you haven't considered (and probably need to hear) is invaluable. We need these gems of truth to learn and grow. This is one of the most powerful ways can we support and learn from each other.

If you're unable receive it from a trusted friend, counselor, or teacher, the Universe is going to rather indelicately throw it in front of you anyway. We will always be offered more chances for self- examination about why we are afraid to speak our truth. Asking yourself some questions can help you discover the reasons.

How did you feel the last time you said something that displeased someone? Why? Do you have a friend who can tell you something you don't want to hear? How do you react? This is where your healing begins. Know you're as worthy as anyone on this planet to have your own voice and to love, love, love yourself no matter what you find there.

It takes courage to speak the honest-to-goodness truth as you see it. It takes a healthy soul and a good dose of self-worth to accept that others may not only dislike what you say but it could result in anger and (gasp) a Twitter war or an unfriending! Each time we smother our voice our light gets a little dimmer. Do this too long and eventually you won't know what you want, who you are, or what you stand for.

So, open up that fifth chakra (communication central) and let it rip from time to time. Speak up, question, have an opinion, offer compassionate counsel. Your voice is important. True spiritual connection is not destroyed by a little honesty. There may be repercussions, but the reward is the peace that comes from being true to yourself. I always trust a person who has the courage to tell me the truth, even when it's difficult to hear.

Do more of that.

Emotion

There's Not as Much Drama in Freedom

*I*t takes a lot of energy to be absorbed in praise-seeking, control games, competition, and the general emotional chaos of a life of extreme sensation. It disrupts our lives and the subsequent drama is felt by those around us. As Obi Wan said, "I feel a great disturbance in the Force!"

For some, experiencing intense pain and/or pleasure in order to feel alive is addictive. In this state, everything feels personal and it's all about you. If drama's not present, you feel the need to stir it up to gain attention or get the rush you crave from extreme emotion. You'll be confined by your emotional demands and unaware of the damage you may be causing in the world and to the people around you.

Going within to increase self-awareness frees you from the roller coaster of out-of-control emotion. It doesn't mean you'll be perfect and immune to damaging situations and sticky feelings, but it does give you the option to choose an honest response and learn from what you're experiencing. It releases you from the cage of exaggerated emotion.

I suppose you could call it response-ability. When put together this sounds like a word we try to avoid, but practicing it helps build the trust you need to take care of yourself and respond as best you can. It's self-preservation at its best. Not just a survival reaction, but the ability to be conscious of the reality of a situation and what your truth tells you is the right course of action. This cuts down considerably on the over-analyzing and emotional obsessing that occurs when you jump on the endless loop of the drama wheel.

Getting off that wheel creates breathing room to find what's true for you. Being honest with yourself and others creates a sense of relief and the possibility of real healing.

Check in to see if, in fact, *you're* the drama queen. Are you communicating your feelings on a regular basis or do you wait and have blowups to release them? Do you feel the need or get pleasure from (or notice someone else does) charging others up to match your intense emotions? Is there a friend who just wears you out with their extremes? Who or what is a calming effect in your life?

Balance in all things.

Do You Know Whose or What Emotion You're Feeling Today?

*I*t's a simple question, but how often do you really ask yourself what emotion you're entertaining? We fling about words and energy, rarely taking the time to slow down and examine what the heck is going on inside of us.

Are you really angry or are you hurt? Are you bored or actually experiencing frustration? Is this depression or are you grieving a loss? I know a few people who can't even identify if they're happy or excited about something.

When you are confused, questioning whether you're mimicking a feeling to please or if you've absorbed emotion from somebody around you will greatly increase your emotional intelligence. You might be having a perfectly productive day and get the inevitable e-mail or phone call from an upset, dumping friend that derails your day. Now you're feeling low and don't know why. What did you take on? I've observed as one angry person spread their energy through an entire room, making everyone there agitated and uncomfortable.

If you practice asking yourself these questions regularly, you become more aware of the difference between your own emotions and when you're actually being affected by something outside yourself.

Keep it simple—ask, "Is this mine or someone else's?"

Survival: An Opportunity for Creation

So, if a bear is chasing you and you're running like crazy to get away, that's survival (first chakra—physical safety, security, and grounding). All your energy will go to staying alive and that's it. Hopefully you're hiking with a slower friend who carries Snickers in their pockets!

But we do experience different levels of this survival experience whenever our comfort is threatened. Anxiety about paying the bills, fear that someone doesn't like you, distress about a career decision, or any number of daily stressors can put you into a lesser form of the fight-or-flight response. Acting defensive, needlessly competing, anger, and a need to control are often actually survival reactions. When you're in this state, nothing seems to go your way. The message you're sending out is fear, confusion, and lack so all your attention and energy will be focused on that and draw more of the same.

Breathe ... the bear is not chasing you! This is perspective time. Why are you giving so much importance to a temporary blip and letting it control your sense of well-being?

Most of the time, a survival response is an indication that something needs to change. You're in a situation you're not comfortable with. Any emotion is a sign pointing to an area in your life that wants some attention and/or growth. A first step is to break the pattern of the survival response you're in before you fall down the rabbit hole into more misery. Change the energy!

If you meditate, do it now. Does a brisk walk in the woods clear your head? Go! Do you do breathing exercises? Inhale, exhale, repeat. Is there a beautiful, uplifting piece of music or art that affects your mood? Call someone who makes you laugh (hopefully at yourself) or try doing something that makes your body feel safe like taking a bath, petting your cat, or eating some pasta. Pretty much anything you can do to entertain a different emotion and energy will pull you up and out of that first chakra so you can regroup.

Once you get a bit more space from what's stimulating the fear and anxiety, you can ask yourself what you'd rather have in your life. Is it time to change or create a new career? Should you let an unhealthy relationship go by the wayside? Do you need to take better care of yourself?

Use survival as an impetus to action. Any action with intent to grow will send those ripples of change out into your life. So, don't worry about it being the right thing—just move. We all go into survival mode, but recognizing it will open the door for you to ask yourself the right question. "Well, if this isn't working ... what will?" Create away!

You Can Have Emotions and Be Neutral at the Same Time

D o you own your emotions or do your emotions own you? If you take time to know what you're feeling, your emotions won't get overblown, out of control, and/or inappropriate to the situation.

Checking in with yourself fast tracks what your emotions are trying to teach you so you can move on more quickly. Your emotions will still be there, but the goal is communication, not destruction. This is you, the spirit, using emotions as a tool for personal growth with no judgement about the experience. It's the higher self at work interpreting the signals from the lower chakras.

When you're stuck in an emotional whirlpool (wallowing in the second chakra), it's painful and the only relief is usually to hurl it out of yourself to those around you in an out-of-proportion way. Unacknowledged emotion usually gets delivered destructively and at the wrong person as the buildup is released.

It may not even be what you really feel and the aftermath makes you reluctant to express yourself again. I bet you've all experienced the effects of "The Big Blow Up." No matter which end of the blow-up you're on, it's shocking and makes you duck from future communication with everyone involved.

It's important to practice listening to and expressing what you're feeling on a regular basis. It dissipates the intensity of the emotion and prevents those unsightly, out-of-control explosions. As you increase self-trust and recognition of what you're feeling, you will value your emotions as a path to growth. Sometimes just identifying what throws you off course will lead to the answer your emotions are pointing to.

Resistance is a Teacher,
Not a Protection

D o you tense up when someone walks into a room whom you don't want to see? Have you experienced a feeling of dread on the way to an event or conversation that you're not looking forward to? You know the feeling: stomach-churning, teeth-clenching, shallow-breathing, feet-dragging resistance. Your mind's saying, "No, no, I don't want to face this/them; you can't make me! This stinks; I won't do it!"

It's a contraction of your energy. It pulls inward and gets small and dense. It's as if we actually take up less space and it doesn't feel good. It's like living in a small cage. We think shrinking back and putting up defensive barriers between us and whatever we're resisting protects us, but if the rules of energy have taught us anything, it's that we attract what we most try to repel. Ever go to a movie and watch the tall guy meandering his way toward your seat as you repeat the mantra, "Not in front of me, not in front of me." Where did he sit?

Resistance is a dense energy that actually creates a magnetic target for what you're trying to avoid—a wall that can be hit. Habitual resistance to an event or person is basically a message that you're not feeling safe. When you perceive a threat, your fight-or-flight mechanism gets activated. Maybe check to see if there are any grizzlies around. If not, relax ... you may be overreacting.

As soon as you become aware you're resisting, ground yourself, breathe deeply, and ask what you're really feeling and why. Is there an action you need to take? Resistance in communication with a friend can mean there's a truth you're afraid to talk about. If you're at (or thinking about) work, maybe you aren't happy with your job or it's a signal you need to deal with an unhealthy pattern or situation.

There's nothing wrong with experiencing resistance and recognizing it as an important step in understanding yourself. It's a normal reaction to danger that helps ensure our survival. But you'll go beyond reaction to self-wisdom when you're candid about why you feel the way you do. Then this emotion can be a tool that points you in the direction of truth to become your own teacher.

You move out of resistance when you gain enough information to feel safe again. So, take some time to notice specific situations or people you often feel resistant to and ask yourself why. Is the resistance protecting you from a different emotion you're reluctant to face?

Just for fun, take a moment, hold your breath and on the count of three resist as hard as you can. One ... two ... three ... hold it, hold it, resist harder with all your might! OK, let it go and take a deep breath. Shrug your shoulders, shake your body out, and realize how silly that was and how good it felt to let it go. Or, you could resist doing this goofy exercise—your choice.

Discernment and Judgement are Not the Same Thing; One of Them is Neutral

iscernment is perceiving truth to gain wisdom; weigh the info and determine a clear choice about your response and actions. Simply put, it answers the question, "Is this the truth or a lie?" It flows from the neutral observer part of you that allows for all things to exist without judgement.

This is a spiritual ability of the sixth, or brow, chakra (clairvoyance or seeing truth beyond the physical realm) and the seventh, or crown, chakra (certainty or knowledge without doubt).

Judgement usually springs from the learned beliefs and concepts that keep the ego safe and determine right or wrong in your world. When the ego is running the show, any information that differs from what it identifies with is a threat and is deemed bad or wrong. This is the essence of judgement: the blanket rejection of another's point of view because it differs from our own

So, when someone's judging your belief, appearance, or choices, it may spring from a place of fear and uncertainty within themselves and an overall disconnect from a spiritual (or bigger) view. When you judge yourself to be a failure or unworthy in some way, you've lost the higher connection reminding you of the infinity of your soul. You're more than this body, this life, this moment. No other being has the right to determine your worth and you will only do that to yourself when you've forgotten the divine light your soul was born from.

Decide that, at least for today, you're fine the way you are and love yourself as is. Even if you don't believe it right now. Be gentle when you notice things you wish to change in yourself. See it as step in your growth, not as self-punishment. Dismiss any thought whispered in your ear with a judgmental voice. Maybe tomorrow and the next day you can hold those thoughts a bit longer.

When Something Sparks Your Enthusiasm, Do it Again!

*E*nthusiasm is a vital, high state of energy that makes us feel alive. It's the excitement and ease you feel when you're completely enjoying yourself. It might be sparked by dancing, hanging out with a cherished friend, singing, baking, painting, writing, or just playing with your dog. It feels timeless with freedom and exhilaration coursing through you. It originates from a Greek word meaning "inspired by God" and is centered in the crown, or seventh, chakra (inspiration, connection to higher consciousness, happiness, seniority).

What creates that sensation for you? Is it a regular part of your life?

Enthusiasm builds on itself and gets stronger the more often you experience it; it's also magnified when you share or match it with someone else. It creates a synergy that reverberates out into the world like ripples in a pond and many a great creation springs forth from a no-holds-barred session of this kind. Repeating any activity or situation that makes you feel this way is like strengthening a muscle; it gets stronger and easier for you to go to that place in yourself

When you're having a "life sucks" day, pull up a memory of the last time you really laughed (amusement is enthusiasm's sister) or felt breathless excitement. Now, even if you aren't able to feel it, take a moment to rebuild the picture of that moment and note the details and who you were with. You'll either start matching the energy in that memory and elevate your mood or at least get a reminder that this too shall pass. If you had enthusiasm before, you'll have it again.

Practice Tolerant Compassion

I t's easy to be compassionate when you aren't getting your buttons pushed but pretty tough to do when you're in disagreement about politics, philosophy, religion, actions, and/or beliefs.

Does that mean we're only loving toward those just like us? Unfortunately, that's how many interpret compassion. I'll give to you and extend a hand if you agree with me and obey my rules (governments love to do that one, as do many religions). I know liberal, vegan Birkenstock wearers and gun-supporting, meat-eating conservatives that are equally judgmental and intolerant of opposing beliefs.

But most great teachers and wisdom traditions have at the core of their teaching a unity and compassion for all things. This is *agape*, or the unconditional love for God and man regardless of the situation. Many seem to have forgotten this. Tolerance is neutrally accepting and allowing for views and beliefs different from our own.

On a good day, through meditation, I find that place of peace and unity where I'm aware of the bigger picture of life and accept things that are not my truth. At times, it allows me to see my past incarnations where I've embodied some of these same opinions and practices I'm judging that are no longer part of who I am in the present.

And then there are those days where I can't find a still moment anywhere and I want to rail against unfairness and cruelty from the rooftops. And I sometimes do! That's why the phrase is "practice" tolerant compassion. It's an ongoing challenge and rich with soul development and wisdom.

This doesn't mean you never take a stand or choose what to believe in. You can stand in your strength, state your position with clarity and truth, and take the action you feel appropriate. But I've never yet seen anyone persuade another to change with hate and anger. They might agree with you out of the fear of being rejected or attacked, but that's bullying, not communication or tolerance. It doesn't matter how right you think you are ... a bully is a bully. Many a war is fought with the motto "God is on our side."

Keep it simple and try to understand and listen without judgement to even one person's position that's different from your own. Maybe next week, listen to another one. This is how we can come together and understand why it is we hold different views and learn from each other. You might not agree, but you can understand.

If everybody did this once a week we could send out a wave of unconditional love that could spread throughout the world.

Neutrality and Apathy are Not the Same Thing

*O*h, who cares. Whatever ... right?

Apathy is a low energy (or absence of energy). It's not fun to be in or around and can suck the life right out of a room. When you're apathetic, not much interests you. There's no enthusiasm or joy in anything and it walks hand in hand with depression. An apathetic person follows the path of least resistance with minimal output and they're easy to manipulate by anyone with a strong will.

Have you ever felt this way? It could be caused by an emotional train wreck, a block on your path, drugs, a blow to the soul, an illness, pain, or even a medication you're on. All of these can stop the natural flow of spiritual energy in your body and shut you down.

Neutrality is being unattached to the result of an emotion or experience; it's not an absence of feeling. You just aren't stuck in any particular spot. It allows freedom of movement and acceptance of all emotions, acknowledging the existence of them as valid. You can feel an emotion and still be neutral as you learn from and accept what you're feeling with no judgment. Emotions are our teachers pointing the way to self-awareness.

Apathy is the loss of connection to the wisdom in our emotions. Ultimately it means you aren't aware of yourself as a spirit and you can't hear your inner voice or the signals from your mind or body. It's far better to feel something than nothing!

If you find yourself in a state of apathy, it could be time to ask what it is you're really feeling. Most apathy is a mask for deeper, spookier emotions we may not feel equipped to handle. Basically, you can't deal with what's coming up, so shutting down seems the best survival move. At this point, any action can help shake you loose from where you're stuck.

If you suspect a physical cause, you could take a walk, quit eating sugar, lay off the pot, get some sleep, check your medications, and/ or go see a doctor or nutritionist you trust for more info.

If it's a spiritual or emotional issue, you'll probably need some sort of sounding board to get clarity about what's bugging you. Open up to a trusted friend or family member; find a good spiritual counselor or therapist to talk to for perspective. Meditate or pray with a friend or group to create a different energy; listen to an online guided meditation or some uplifting music.

Physical, mental, and spiritual causes aren't really separate, but sometimes addressing one gets everything to move. Simply owning up to being apathetic may be enough for you to decide it's not where you want to be and get things moving again.

Balance

Enlightenment Can Happen
Reaching for Frozen Peas
at the Supermarket

*Y*ou laugh, but I've had some version of that happen to me many times. I do some of my best work in grocery stores. Well, maybe I haven't found total enlightenment, but I have come across answers to problems I'm having.

Have you ever used laser-like focus, concentrating with all your might as you search for the answer to a problem? The harder you try, the more stuck you get. Finally, throwing your hands up in frustration you go, "Forget it, I'm going to the movies!" and there, munching on popcorn in the dark, some image or story leads to your answer. You found the answer by letting it go.

When you struggle to be anyplace other than where you are it's avoidance, and it's a good bet those wheels you're spinning will stay stuck where they are. Acceptance brings you into the present moment so action is again possible.

Since spiritual growth is not a linear, problem-solving journey, willing myself to consciousness has never seemed to help—I haven't been able to think my way to spiritual ascension yet! So, if you meditate trying to force a deeply spiritual experience or some particular result, you'll feel like you've failed.

You can't set up goals for enlightenment like you're training for a marathon. No matter how many affirmations and chants you recite or Zen Buddhist koans you read, you can't force it. This is what frustrates many beginning meditators as the laws of mind and body don't necessarily apply to spiritual enlightenment.

Now, anything can be a catalyst and I'm all for finding pearls of wisdom wherever you can. It all works and it all doesn't—depends on where your consciousness is at the moment. But sometimes you just have to let it be and quit trying to get somewhere or find the answer.

Many years ago, I was perusing the metaphysical section of a bookstore desperately seeking the secret of the Universe from some master or another to bail me out. As I pulled out a book I heard a clatter as something fell to the floor. I reached down and picked it up ... I'd found a key!

I started giggling and when the shop owner asked if she could help me I grandiosely said, "No, I'm good; I did, after all, find the Key!" I was in dire need of humor. I mistakenly assumed the more profound and pious my spiritual path, the further I'd get. To "lighten up" was the truth I stumbled on that day, though the store owner didn't seem to find it amusing!

Enlightenment is not another grade, degree, or achievement to be acquired. It can sneak up on you in those quiet times during the most mundane of experiences ... even buying frozen peas. Effortless being and appreciating right where we are in the moment is the quiet truth of enlightenment.

What are You Aware of Now?
And Now … How About Now?

You've heard it many ways: be in the moment, stop and smell the roses, present time, carpe diem! So, are you aware of your surroundings—what's happening and what you're feeling right now? We think we're present, but our mind is chattering away (like little monkeys) about what's next on the daily agenda. In the middle of a conversation with another actual human, you wander off. "I'm so sorry to hear about your husband/children/ job/illness." *What should I pick up for dinner and who's texting me?*

Let's face it … you probably just drifted off reading this.

Breathe, shrug your shoulders a couple times, and stop. No, I mean it, just breathe and sit there for a moment. Where are you? Are you warm, cold, tired, happy, sad, or frustrated? Check in with yourself and see what's real in your universe at this moment. No judgement. You don't even have to try and fix anything; just observe what's up.

It works the same if you want to deepen and improve your relationships. Really look at and listen to who is in front of you. It's rare enough now to have a face-to-face moment with someone without technology between us. You can miss so much worrying about the future and rehashing the past. This moment is a gift; don't waste it. It passes sooner than you think.

So... what's up with you right now?

Without the Inner Balance of Spirit, We Just Keep Falling Down

*B*alance is the thing. Every single day is like walking a tight wire to keep the various parts of our life going. Health, good relationships, satisfying career, family, emotional needs, spiritual practice, and chores all demand our attention. We rapidly switch from one to the other according to what screams the loudest. In a blink, you can find yourself losing your balance and focusing most of your attention on one or more of these needs and neglecting others.

If there's no time for you to be still and check in with your deepest self, you just keep running until ... bam! You run into a wall that most annoyingly points out where you neglected an important part of your life. This could be a health scare, a hurt friend, financial disaster, or an injury. You may have made a mistake at work or had an emotional meltdown. At any rate, your harmony is lost.

A daily spiritual practice of some kind quiets everything down so you can hear and see your priorities and give yourself a head start to regain your footing in the face of unexpected events. It's good to train yourself in times of stability so you're ready to handle those uncontrollable events and the stress that's sure to pop up.

A friend of mine who excels in martial arts told me she goes through daily mental and physical discipline so when a skill is needed, there's an effortless response of correct action that returns her equilibrium.

Checking in with yourself each day can avoid a lot of the mistakes, poor decisions, and problems in your life. Even the smallest time out can slow you down enough to regain balance and continue on.

Take a break.

Don't Give Too Much to Those Who Don't Give to Anyone Else

*I*deally things get passed forward in life. I kindly open the door for you and the next day you open a door for someone else, making the world a more hospitable place. It may not work that directly, but kindness for its own sake is a healthy principle to live by.

The Native American Potlatch (give-away ceremony) practices this by freely giving away a valuable or useful item to another with no regret or attachment and receiving a blessing in the giving. It's healthy to give because you choose to, without expectation of return

However, it can become important to draw a line if you're giving to people who are repeatedly selfish and unkind to others, a.k.a. the takers. You can get drained by those who are self-centered, unconscious, and motivated by their own gain. These are often very charming people, and in some cases, professional victims, that you'll find yourself continuously bailing out. They won't cover your back, don't help others unless it benefits them, and become entitled to your generosity. Whatever you do, it doesn't really change anything for them and if you stop giving they simply move on to someone else who'll play the game.

If you find you're in a repetitive situation and feel taken from and depleted, it's time to examine not only their motives but perhaps your own pattern and expectation in the giving. Being conscious of your choices can break the cycle you may be caught in. Your desire to give to others might be better served elsewhere.

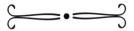

Tell-tale signs of this pattern: Do you feel tired after being with certain friends? Are you often pulled away from your plans to attend to someone else's wants and needs? Have you been getting cranky and complaining about how much you give to a friend, family member etc.? Spend more time with those who value you and contribute to raising you (and others) up and less with the takers.

Feed the Soul, Starve the Ego

Well, we of course need an ego to function and relate to the society we're in. We don't, however, need to make it the overfed monster it's become.

When disconnected from the voice of spirit, all we can hear is the craving to be recognized as OK. Running frantically down the soul-depleting path of external validation we seek approval, physical success, and the adulation of others. It puts us in competition with each other in destructive ways.

Take a clear look at some of the so-called role models we revere in our culture. A beloved television father who has destroyed many women's lives, a brilliant comedian who took his own life in despair, a talented athlete lying about drug use in order to keep winning. These are people we admired who lost their footing to the screaming need of the ego. If ego is not tempered by the soul, it can lead us onto dark paths. It's a lonely, sad, and often angry place to live and is ultimately tragic evidence of a loss of spiritual connection.

When you take the time to listen to the voice of the soul (God, the Supreme Being, The Big Giant Head, the Universe, etc.) you'll feel the emanation of spirit in you and everyone. Compassion, understanding, and love are present and while alone, you are not lonely.

Feeding the spirit means taking some portion of your day to meditate, pray, chant, commune with nature, or read an uplifting book to contemplate something bigger than your daily life. It doesn't matter what religion you are or aren't, it's a commitment to yourself when you focus on activities that deepen your connection to spirit and strengthen your soul.

When you have this spiritual balance, the ego gets used in its proper role as interpreter between the soul and the body. It assists you in expressing through your creations who you are out into the world.

Every part of us has a role in contributing to our soul experiencing and learning from the human experience.

Spirit Knows When to Be Still and When to Pick Up the Knife

I was struggling with a volatile situation that caused the end of communication with a friend. I spent months trying to repair it: owning my part, apologizing, and consistently attempting to fix it even though the fault was shared. Eventually wanting the punishment to end, I trashed myself by taking full responsibility for the problem. All attempts were met with rejection and silence.

One night I dreamt I was a little child riding in a big yellow school bus. A group of mean girls were yelling and making fun of me as I got smaller and smaller, cowering in my seat. Taking their words like blows I cried, "Why don't you like me?"

I felt a warm presence beside me and turned to see an old, wrinkled Native American man with a red bandana tied around his head staring at me. The light from his piercing eyes looked right into my soul, but no one else seemed to notice him. As the muted sound of their abuse faded into the background, he pushed a knife toward me blade first and quietly said, "Sometimes you must pick up the knife."

Shrinking back from him I whispered, "I can't; I'm afraid it'll hurt me!"

"Could it hurt worse than that?" he said as he gestured with the blade toward the mean girls. He opened my hand and turned the knife so the handle rested in my palm. "There's a time to fight and a time to be still. You'll know how to choose when the time is right. Trust yourself." When I looked up from my hand, he was gone. The girls now stood silently staring at the blade I held. They turned without a word and returned to their seats as if nothing had happened, and I awoke.

I've often revisited the wisdom in that dream. A reminder to own my power and not fear standing up for myself and others. There are times you'll need to marshal forces within you to do what needs to be done, walk away when necessary, release responsibility for what isn't yours, and speak out when called for. Picking up the knife says you will not accept destruction to your soul from anyone. Owning the power in that decision creates a stillness in you that speaks far louder that any aggression could.

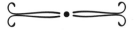

Are you afraid to stand up to a person or situation that's making you feel small? What do you need to release that keeps you from loving and protecting yourself? If you're fearful in a social situation, what are you feeling or witnessing that threatens your well-being? What do you want to do about it?

Get Over it! Did I Mention ... Get Over it!

*L*et's talk about your problems, shall we? Oh, wait, let's not! I know, there's a time and place for discussing your life events with a trusted friend or counselor, but good grief, at some point you have to move on.

We all need compassion about our issues and we have different rates of growth and recovery. So yes, we need to be patient about each other's problems. But when does hearing and/or talking about it repeatedly just become a reinforcement of the pain we're in? It's possible to rebuild the problem and emotion of an event each time you revisit it and never really let it go.

Words and mental images hold and draw energy. If enough well-intentioned, sympathetic people enable the broken-record approach to healing, it can reinforce the problem. You'll always be able to find "pain buddies" to compare notes with about the lousy situation you're in. Misery loves company, but surrounding yourself with negative energy will make you stay miserable forever. You can all stay stuck together or seek out a different vibration to match and move up out of the mire.

Don't get so attached to your damage that you form your identity around it and start to believe it's who you are. Unless you decide to move past the place you're in and move on to the next opportunity for change, you'll always be looking out the window at the same landscape.

I once saw a Bob Newhart skit on Mad TV where he was a five-dollar therapist. After people unloaded their many problems on him he'd look up smile and loudly yell "Stop it!" Flustered, they insistently went on trying to get sympathy for their woes. He calmly listened and when they finished would again shout, "Stop it!" Sometimes, that may be just what you need to say to yourself.

That'll be five dollars, please.

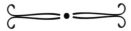

There's a fine line between wallowing and healing. Do you know the difference in yourself? Can you see that pattern in others? Do you shy away from those who don't commiserate with your pain and reject friends who offer real wisdom and insight to help you move on?

Relationships

Consider the Possibility That You Picked Your Parents

A wise man once told me if you asked yourself why you picked your parents, you could learn everything there was to know about yourself. Even if you don't believe in reincarnation, just considering the complex and multilayered relationship we have with our families can underline what our soul is here to learn.

What are the biggest challenges in your relationship to your mother? How about your father? What are the gifts you got from each? Where do you appreciate the behaviors you inherited and which ones do you resist and vow never to do?

Are you in a romantic relationship that mimics your parents' or is it a model of doing the opposite? Did your family teach you to communicate your feelings and beliefs openly or did they repress it and criticize because "that's who we are?" Do you have different goals and a lifestyle created by you, or are you struggling to find identity separate from their goals and limitations?

Complicated, isn't it? Good or bad, our relationship to our parents is rich with learning about life and the path we picked to be on. Many never question this relationship and go along with the status quo, reflecting the beliefs and influence of the family agreement.

Not questioning that reality is particularly harmful to a spirit who picked a difficult and abusive family stuck in self-destructive patterns. We often choose the tough ones as impetus for self-introspection and to separate from a truth that's not ours. At times this is karmic in nature and leads to even greater awareness of our past lives, the spiritual realm, and how it works in our current life.

I don't believe we all necessarily had the awareness of this choice between lifetimes and some souls do get caught in energy and situations they were not consciously choosing. Nonetheless, if you survive it, you can still use it to reclaim your power and own the growth from whatever you experienced.

When you question and examine family relationships, the possibilities are rich for growth and change for the whole group. Letting go of expectation and simply enjoying (or not) the differences between you and your family creates the space to communicate, forgive, love, and enjoy each other.

Remember that no family is perfect. It is what it is, the agony and the ecstasy.

A True Friend Will Take the Hard Road with You and Tell You the Painful Truth

*F*riends come and go in life. We have work friends, coffee buddies, Facebook friends, and those we share hobbies with. It's good to pepper our lives with different kinds of friends on a variety of levels. But don't we all need that friend who will tell us when we have spinach in our teeth? These honest, deep friendships are few and far between.

Unfortunately, many people aren't even sure what a good friend looks like or how to be one. You know the kind I mean—that dynamic soul-to-soul contact that defies logic and fulfills a part of your life. They could be a kindred spirit from a past life connection or a present-time companion with shared interests: a spiritual running buddy, so to speak. They've seen you at your worst and best and still stick around. Late at night, stuck and miserable, you can call them and they'll listen to you, even if they've heard it all before. They're joyful about your successes, encourage you to get up when you fail, and include you in their most significant moments.

A true friend isn't perfect and doesn't expect you to be. If you hurt them, they forgive you, remembering that the good of the relationship outweighs the bad. They don't abandon you when life falls apart and tend to take your side if someone hurts you. If your behavior or blind spots create drama, they'll help point out what you're stuck on. You share laughter with and about each other. These are the friends you trust to tell you when you've made a foolish move.

Sounds pretty good, doesn't it? Well, the reason we don't have a lot of those is because this quality of friendship requires commitment, time, and shared experience. It develops because of the mutual trust that builds from that. Consequently, we don't have room or time in our lives for an abundance of those. You'll need to decide at some point who's going to occupy a spot that important in your life.

Who do you trust to be core support, buoy up your life, and give you a soft place to land in times of trouble? It's an honor to be and have a true friend. It thrives when cherished and breaks our heart when destroyed.

If you have a lack of true friends in your life, consider applying these attributes to the relationship you have with yourself. The most important friendship to nourish and count on is the one you have with you. Treat yourself as you would a trusted pal. This actually increases your discernment and sense of self-worth and helps you choose your companions more wisely, bypassing those who drop you at the first sign of trouble.

However, it is important to have friends of all types. Sometimes all you need is the light friendship you have in a situational contact like a happy hello shared with your favorite barista or bantering with a companion sweating away in Zumba class. They might be temporary and fleeting, but they spark the spirit-to-spirit connection that knows no time or space and makes you feel less alone.

Remember, it's quality not quantity.

If you aren't sure what you want in a good friendship, notice what you admire in the ones you see around you. If in doubt about how to do be a true friend, I suggest you adopt a dog. They are, after all, the experts on this.

Karma is No Excuse

*I*t's my karma to be unhappy. I was bad in a past life; I'm suffering now because it's what I deserve. It's our karma to be together. I've heard all of these statements about the mysterious effects of karma. To many, it's the what-goes-around-comes-around theory of life.

It's all about forgiving yourself and moving on. If you believe the previous statements, you'll get stuck in the position of needing to suffer in order to forgive your karma. You can get caught up in a belief or situation you recreate (yes, it can be from lifetime to lifetime) because you've not forgiven yourself or another and reclaimed your energy to focus it in a new direction. Karma is not a spiritual principal to use as an excuse or to point at others with the claim that its's their own fault and they somehow deserve it. After all ... it's *their* karma.

If you're having an inexplicable attraction or repulsion to someone you just met or there's a pattern you seem to play out repeatedly, it could be karmic. If it is, ask yourself what you didn't learn the first time and set about awakening to the knowledge you need to release it in the present. You can reclaim your spiritual, creative energy in the present and create something new from freedom.

Not everything is karmic and happening to balance things out for good or bad. Could be you just weren't paying attention and made an unconscious choice or you needed to learn a particular lesson and in your higher spiritual wisdom created the perfect situation to learn from.

Want to release? Imagine a simple image in front of you of an unfinished circle and fill it up with the karma you wish to complete. See it as a color if that's easier for you. Once it's full, complete the circle and watch it dissolve as if it's dust being blown away in the wind. Forgive yourself and forgive others.

It Takes a Powerful Person to Extend Mercy

*I*n the past, I thought it a sign of weakness and a loss of power to forgive someone. I've since learned that hanging onto anger and resentment is a terrible feeling and it weakens your soul. No matter how you justify it by replaying the offense done to you, it'll never feel good. Fantasizing about harm coming their way or finally winning that argument you have with them in your head vents emotion, but ultimately feeds the wound.

Mercy is forgiveness, compassion, and clemency extended when you have the power to punish someone.

I once had my heart broken by a betrayal from a friend who knew a great deal about my life, strengths, fears, and weaknesses. Due to her own broken soul, she destroyed our friendship in a dramatic way and it was the instant end of our connection. It was difficult to understand or accept but it opened up a path of personal growth that made me a stronger, wiser person.

Years later I saw this woman at an event trying to curry the favor of some acquaintances of mine that I had a healthy relationship with. I took a deep breath and at that moment decided I didn't want to feel that sense of dread anymore and walked up to say hello. I addressed the group with, "This is a very talented woman." Turning to face her I said, "It's nice to see you again." She threw her arms around me in relief saying how great it was to see me.

After a bit more polite discussion I moved on and as I walked away said to myself," And that's who you are!" I felt a tremendous release and healing as I chose mercy instead of retribution. That choice was for me. It freed me from resentment and finished repairing the hurt and damage to my self-worth that the situation had caused.

I wouldn't have had the strength to do that a few years before. It underlined for me how far I'd come and affirmed the kind of person I wish to be in the world. But I couldn't let go of it until I was ready. Be gentle with yourself if you're not quite ready to let go. You can't force forgiveness; it has its own timetable.

If you want to injure someone who hurt you, stop and ask yourself who really loses and who gains if you take revenge. Are you damaging yourself by holding onto old anger about a past situation? A bit of your soul is darkened when you destroy anything or anyone. Light pours in when you choose to respond from the strength of compassion and the desire to be free of old pain.

If the Best You Can Hope for is to Not be Damaged ... Move on

A good buddy of mine stopped by to share a pot of tea after attending what was supposed to be a relaxing lunch at a winery with an old friend. She dragged herself in, plopped down on the couch, and commenced whining about her shortcomings and failures. I said, "Oh, you must have been at lunch with (name omitted to protect the guilty). Why do you spend time with her?" I noticed after each conversation or outing with this particular woman, she felt bad about herself and considered it a victory if she came out unscathed.

Her review of the day started with a gushing "I'm so happy to see you!" and progressed to a monologue about her life. "You have allergies; I never have allergies. Have you heard about this product that helps you lose belly fat? You might want to check it out. I feel sorry for people who don't have children (she does—my friend doesn't)."

It was a running commentary on her perfect life and where she was "winning." Real feelings were rarely discussed, unless she needed counseling on what someone else had done to her. My friend felt invisible and when she shared about her own life there was no interest. In the course of the lunch her mood would plummet from the numerous digs and afterwards she had to either put herself back together or, at best, felt bored. Have you had a friendship like that?

It's not uncommon to remain attached to friendships we've outgrown. Some of them become obsolete as we grow and change, particularly if the connection was fashioned from a mutual need, belief, or pattern that's no longer current. They may have been formed while still healing from childhood damage and play out in destructive ways. At times, they're karmic in nature and challenge you to grow and face things about yourself.

It takes a lot of compassion to understand that this kind of competitive behavior is reflecting a lack of self-worth, but that still doesn't mean you have to stay "on the line" and receive abuse.

As you learn what a healthy, supportive friendship is (as we discussed earlier), you can choose to focus your time and attention on relationships where you both thrive. You'll no longer need to hang out with friends where the best outcome at lunch is boredom and the worst is destruction. You can choose to understand and put up with their behavior, have a heart-to-heart talk about it, or move away from the relationship.

The next time you notice your energy feels low after spending time with a friend, ask if this happens frequently. Do you feel listened to and supported? Are you expecting to feel bad and dreading seeing them? If the answer is yes, it may be time to move away from that old friendship and pay more attention to friends you feel good with.

Never Regret Loving Someone; It's a Noble Thing, Regardless of the Outcome

hough it is a bit of a cliché, you do learn something from everyone you've ever loved. Even if it's to not make the same mistake twice.

It takes courage and openness of spirit to own up to loving someone. It's a commitment to the deepest part of you and the intense desire that drives the soul to share and connect. Spooky stuff for us humans. What if it isn't reciprocated or it goes away? What if you don't deserve love? What if there just isn't anyone there?

If you started out life in a difficult family situation or have been hurt in the past, these questions torment you when you reach out. This can lead you to seek out someone else to fill you up with love so you feel worthy or cause you to pick people incapable of healthy love because you think that's what you deserve. It's a dangerous loss of power when you seek external approval to feel better about yourself.

It's worth the risk, though, as each foray into love teaches us what it's really all about. It's a gift to find that place of peace where you aren't trying to give love in order to be loved, but can experience the joy and appreciation for another that's unconditional love. You don't expect anything from them and feel happiness about their mere existence in this world.

Learning to be fulfilled by loving yourself first gives you the freedom to share affinity with others from a place of abundance rather than lack or need. It might take some time to learn how to do this and discover what it feels like, so be patient with yourself. Every relationship that seems like a failure is really practice for how to truly have an intimate, loving connection.

There are always more people to love so if you're ready, let go and open your heart for the next lesson. Once when I was suffering from a heartbreak a co-worker said to me, "You know, a new bus stops by every five minutes!"

Whether they stay in your life or not, if you've had that feeling it stretches the heart and increases your capacity to give and receive love. That's a noble action for the soul, no matter the outcome.

Who are You Playing Games With? Chess Anyone?

*G*ames are fun when you play them for sport, testing your skill and socializing with others. They're not so healthy when they're part of your relationships.

Games in relationships can manifest in passive-aggressive behavior, bullying, playing the victim, controlling behavior, and manipulation. If you're hiding from your feelings, unable to face pain and anger and connect with others, you'll probably adopt some of these behaviors to express yourself or even seek them out in others.

Relationship games destroy trust and are about making the right move to win, not about increasing connection and intimacy. Strategy is good in war games and sports but can destroy love. Keep your gamesmanship for the playing field or on the chess board. You'll always feel unsafe in a relationship filled with games instead of real love and support.

You get to make the decision about what qualities you want in those you interact with and which ones you want to develop in yourself. Write loyalty, humor, honesty, commitment, compassion, generosity, support, and forgiveness at the top of the list.

Perfecting relationships is not the same as perfecting your game.

If you want healthy relationships, it's time for a dose of honesty. Are you engaging in relationship games and who are you playing them with? Is this the type of communication you want to have? Who aren't you being honest with? Why? Are you having any fun?

If You Need to be Right, Your Ego is Running the Show

*H*ow often in the past week have you been in a discussion where you needed others to agree with you or admit you were right?

The ego is our sense of self in the world and in a way, the interpreter of who you are as a spirit reflected in the particular incarnation you're currently living. It's a mediator between the soul and body for successful interaction with others and creates a sense of self-esteem so we can function in the outside world.

When the ego dominates us and is no longer a tool of the spirit, it has a constant need for its existence to be validated in order to feel real and OK. There's no higher self driving the bus at that point, just the noisy kid sitting in the back, running the show and yelling for attention!

When that happens, we find value by getting agreement from those around us that we're on the right track. Disagreement threatens our identity. There will be a right and a wrong side to everything and your success is determined by how well you match the external standards set by those around you.

When your spiritual connection is restored, you can see all sides and step out of the judgement of any one position; self-worth is no longer determined by those around you. When you're filled with your own light you feel at peace, fulfilled, and OK just the way you are. This makes it much easier to appreciate the differences between you and others instead of needing to change them to validate the choices you've made. We need the ego to function in the world, but as a part of the whole of who you are and not as the dictator.

So ... do you think I'm right or wrong?

Ego check: Do you feel diminished or angry if others don't agree with you and can you only enjoy the company of those who share the same opinions? In a discussion, are you busy judging or competing with their words?

If you're all revved up in an ego battle, try this; put the palm of your hand on the solar plexus (a little above the belly button) and gently pat or slowly make small circles with your hand. Muster as much amusement as you can and quietly say to yourself, "I am not going to die if I don't win, I'm ok!" There's a reason mothers instinctively do this to babies when they are stressed. It calms you down and will give you enough of a break to get your balance back and ask where you're coming from.

Inner Voice

Who or What are You Listening to Today?

What voice dominates your thoughts this fine day? Is it the whisper of insecurity and old criticism? Perhaps it sounds like a scolding parent in your head or the chatter of comparison to determine whether you measure up to or surpass another. Are too many shoulds driving you to constant self-improvement? Have you been worrying about imagined symptoms from the latest online mystery illness or seething about the inflammatory politics of some pundit on the news?

Why, oh why, is the quiet, loving voice of your own soul the last one listened to? The cacophony from all this input and stimulation can smother the sound of your own spiritual voice, keeping you from inner harmony.

At some point, you may choose to silence all that racket by disconnecting with substance abuse or any obsessive behavior that takes all your focus and dulls the noise. However, every time you return, the racket will still be there, maybe even louder. Is it any wonder people walk around out of their bodies, spacing out, making poor decisions, and feeling more frustrated every day? Who or what are you letting dominate your thoughts? What messages are you repeating about yourself in your head that aren't true?

It's important to clear out the riffraff and fill your mind with the clear, peaceful voice of your own spirit so you can hear what's right for you. The rest is just noise.

As an experiment, minimize outside stimulus for a day, an hour or even just ten minutes. That means no phones, texting, computers, radio, TV, or even conversations. Find a quiet spot to sit outside if you can. Enjoy the birds, the wind and whatever nature provides. Close your eyes, breathe and be aware of what's around you, gradually focusing your attention to what's gently coming to the forefront within you. It may play out as if you are watching a little movie in your head or listening to the comforting, soft voice of counsel. Hear that?... It's you.

Hmmm ... Excessive Pondering

W hy is that the answer? Am I doing this right? What if I make a mistake? I might be wrong! Are they lying? What are they thinking about me? Wait a minute ... why is that the answer?

It's exhausting to get caught up in an analytical cycle of questions and speculations never answered to your satisfaction. Side effects include anxiety, insecurity, sleeplessness, massive assumption, self-doubt, loss or gain in appetite, and a generally bad attitude.

You're thinking too much, and when the mind takes over, you may need physical activity to shift the energy. It's my experience that when you're stuck in this way, it's difficult to sit down and meditate. It turns into an analyzing, problem-solving session. Go do something and revisit the issue later once you've shifted your focus and energy.

If you find yourself intensely focused on a problem to the point of constant repetition, I prescribe any diversion that changes your attention. Yes, at this moment, distraction is the prescription.

Go to the movies, ride a bike, do Tai Chi in the park, plant some flowers, be of service to someone else, exercise, or eat some chocolate. You'll have a fresh perspective and a bigger view when you revisit the situation later. You might even be able to meditate!

Communication from the Spirit is Often Quiet

The voice of your soul doesn't scold or give you advice. It's the simple, quiet counselor you hear when you slow down enough to listen.

If you're struggling for answers, your head is probably filled with the confusing input and energy of whatever (or whoever) is the loudest. Your inner voice may be whispering guidance to you but it's drowned out by all the hubbub. That voice isn't always literal, however, and frequently will speak to you through the words and actions of others and the world around you. If it's your truth it won't be confusing and you'll feel more centered because of it.

I was once experiencing one of those dark and stormy nights of the soul. My thoughts were full of past regrets and obsessed with future worries as I tried to force a path of willful action. I absently meandered into my backyard, fretting about my problems, and started to hand water the vegetable garden. Zoned out with water bubbling out the end of the hose, a hummingbird dropped in front of me, suspended in midair. I held my breath, watching his little iridescent body hover inches from my face, delicately taking quick sips from the running water. I felt a wisp of air as another bird swooped in, then one more and I was now the water fountain for a family of hummingbirds.

I was spellbound by the slight whirring sound of their wings and felt joy to be of service providing for these happy little beings. The first arrival flew close to my eyes, examining me for a moment, his head turning side to side as he weighed the risk. I felt a brief tickle as he landed on my hand for an instant before winging off to another adventure. After a few beats, thirst quenched, the other two also flew away.

With a lighter heart, I continued nourishing my garden, lingering in that moment of peace. I couldn't recall what thoughts had been so unsettling a few minutes before.

Pay attention and be open to receiving communication in unexpected ways: a quiet thought, conversation with a friend, a stranger's smile, music, or even a bird. If you ask for help, you'll get it. Be still a moment and hear the quiet voice of spirit in your day.

Think, Talk, Get Advice, Analyze, and Talk and Think Some More

elax, quit looking outside yourself for answers and listen to yourself.

Nuff said.

It's Exhausting Trying to be Perfect; Just Do Your Best and Please Yourself

Often, I hear people say with great pride that they're very competitive and need to win. In sports or contests that's an appropriate goal. It's a gauge of comparative excellence. But in your personal life, striving for perfection can become a stick used to beat yourself up. If you never feel good enough, you're always running toward the ever-changing finish line of self-acceptance.

The perfection we think we need to attain can become an arbitrary set of rules with unobtainable goals that seem impossible to achieve. Particularly if they're someone else's standards, approval, or achievement that we're aiming for. Learn to let go of perfection; doing the best you can in any endeavor however is deeply satisfying when it comes from the enthusiasm of the soul.

I played this out in a simple way by starting an exercise regime at the gym. As I was plodding away on a treadmill, the inevitable super runner got on the one next to me. In short order, he cranked it up to a fast run, feet pounding, sweat flying, and I, of course, started bumping up my speed.

Great incentive to work harder, you say? Nope. I felt embarrassed and judged that I wasn't doing enough. Never mind I'd been a couch potato the past year and my heart was pounding like crazy. I was in a competition (albeit an imaginary one) and had to keep up. So, my legs were hurting and I was in agony, hating every minute, until I clearly heard my body say, "If you don't ease up I'm never doing this again!"

I slowed it down until I could comfortably breathe and find a pace I could live with. I became aware of the rhythmic movement of my arms and legs and as I started enjoying the exercise, I forgot about those around me and moved it up a notch to challenge myself. I could only do my best, not the super runner's best, and I felt invigorated and enthused about returning for more.

Doing your best for yourself is a satisfying feeling. Trying to do someone else's best hurts.

Be honest with yourself and ask what you really wish to accomplish and why? Is it your voice answering or someone else's? If yours; what steps can you reasonably take right now to head in that direction? Remember to appreciate each, small, personal success and don't be hard on yourself if you don't get there today. There's another opportunity tomorrow.

When You Need Perspective, Microcosm Reflects Macrocosm and Vice Versa

*W*e're part of and connected to the creation of the world we live in. This is a philosophy in all great spiritual teachings of the world and most recently in the discovery of string theory in physics. You can't really separate what's going on around you from what's going on within you.

When I decide to run errands and I'm in a cranky, irritated space, I can't find parking spaces, drivers cut me off, grocery cashiers are unfriendly, and dogs want to bite me. The environment starts to reflect what I'm expecting and radiating. On the other hand, when I'm feeling peaceful and present in my life, the world looks friendlier and things tend to go much smoother.

Even if the exact same things happen to me, my response is kinder and what I put out transmutes what I experience. In this case my microcosm (small world) has affected the macrocosm (great world). You can often see what's going on inside of someone by looking at what they're manifesting in their lives. The part reflects the whole. You've got to love those Greek philosophers!

We can't control everything that happens to us, but we can control our response to it in our microcosm. Everything and everyone can at times affect us but our response to what happens can also change the macrocosm and the energy in those events we experience. This is the power and the beauty of it. Can you change your life? Absolutely, but you can't necessarily control the exact outcome of that change in the grand scheme of things.

In the larger world, we bemoan wars, poverty, hunger, and the general suffering of mankind, tending to blame it on other people, governments, or religions. Why does it never end? Is the shadow we see in the world the unexamined darkness and spiritual imbalance of our own humanity—our own little world of judgement and anger reflecting into the macro world?

Even when preaching fairness for all, I watch as incredible judgement and anger is expressed toward those don't share the correct politics. This is done in the name of justice and enforcing fairness. But guess what's showing up around us? It's the same energy as the perceived enemy who's just as certain they're right.

You can't hide from the macrocosm; it's within us. Dichotomies will destroy the world until we figure out this opposition comes from us and you cannot force peace with anger or love with hatred.

There's a quote from the seven principles of Hermes that says it best: "As above, so below, as within, so without." I can't solve the problems of the world outside me, but I can choose to find peace and kindness within me and reflect it into the world as best I can to start the ball rolling. Don't like what's around you? Start by examining what's within you. If we all do this, it will surely change the world.

What would it be like to take a day off from judging each other?

Distraction, the Denial of Choice

istraction is a popular choice when we don't want to acknowledge a reality that distresses us in some way. We're remarkably adept at avoiding these situations—numbing ourselves in a multitude of ways until we're too unconscious to even remember something hurts.

You can dwell on emotional dramas and imaginary problems or spend endless hours worrying about any number of disastrous scenarios. Rehashing past catastrophes easily becomes the distraction of choice to justify why you can't move on in your life.

What do you use for distraction when you just can't face your life situation? Is it food, drugs, computers, exercise, partying, work, video games, shopping, sex, drinking, television, gossip, your family, etc.? You could even become a professional seeker, going to yet another new-age workshop or miracle healer to fix it for you.

It can all give you a Band-Aid or provide a piece of the puzzle for your growth. But ultimately much of it is a distraction from the basic, real spiritual work of sitting your butt down, looking at your life, and dealing with it. The answer comes when you ask yourself the right question.

What is your method of distracting yourself and what are you trying to deny exists?

Are You Standing in the Shallow or Deep End of the Pool?

*I*f you want to be intimate and real with people, at some point you're going to feel vulnerable and afraid. This is stepping into the deep end of the pool. It's going within and exposing feelings, beliefs, fears, and flaws that are your total package. It's where true soul-to-soul connection happens.

Trust. If you want to experience the deeper emotions of life and contemplate the more profound philosophies, you'll have to take the plunge and trust. Trust that you'll survive, that someone will catch you, that you're lovable, that your feelings are valid. Trust that you are fine the way you are. At the very least trust that you can float!

I almost drowned as a child in the deep end of a swimming pool and even as an adult who could swim was terrified of water that went over my head. On a trip to Hawaii with my husband we decided to try snorkeling to feed the beautiful tropical fish. Terrified, I stood shaking as he took my hands and gently pulled me through the water. "Trust me, I won't let you drown."

I floated in the waist-deep water, putting my snorkeled face in and marveling at how clear it was. Soon I noticed a breathtaking array of colorful fish in a swirl beneath me as my husband handed me a bag of peas to feed them. I was giggling like a child as they swam up to touch my fingers. It was then I realized we were probably in thirty feet of water!

The shallow end of the pool is fine. You don't think too much or take emotional risks. You can splash around, have some light fun, and avoid anything that causes you to feel too deeply. Sometimes there's a lot to be said for wading around in that end. So, don't judge yourself if that's where you need to be. Recognizing where you're standing is often growth enough. If you get bored though, come on in a bit deeper and see how much more there is beneath the surface. The water is fine.

Marco ...

Some Faint at the First Sign of Truth

I always believed if you're honest, people will be honest back. However, I eventually discovered that there are different versions of honesty. Some are based on fear, insecurity, the need for safety or to feed the ego. At times, honesty can hinge upon the image we want to portray. These are strong influences on how you perceive and express your truth.

A great deal of acceptance comes into play to let people hold the version of truth they need to survive. There's a fine line between understanding someone else's personal truth and judging it as faulty because it's not your own.

It takes a courageous soul to dig deep and face the lies you tell yourself, and you'll need a bucket load of self-love, a strong ability to laugh at yourself, and nonstop letting go. Definitely not an activity for the faint of heart! It's hard to dump a belief or position you've identified with and clung to for years. You may have built that sucker into an iron-clad reality your world revolves around, fearful that facing it could separate you from friends and family.

Any new perspective that doesn't correspond with what we hold true will cause huge stress and discomfort, and we'll do almost anything to drown it out and keep our balance. Even if it means hanging on to untrue, destructive internal beliefs like, "You're stupid and unlovable" or "You'll never be successful." Apply consciousness here: put a new message in the rotation saying something positive.

Since it's pretty destabilizing to be honest with yourself and release self-limiting, out-of-date illusions, it's a good time to relax and lean into the change. Present time is a good friend here and can help you accept the new perspective and freedom, moving you into an expanded reality. When blinders are removed, it's shocking to see how much bigger the world is than the small picture you focused on.

When I was fourteen I was spending the night at a friend's who asked me to go to church with her family the next morning. All I knew at that point was Catholicism; her church was full Gospel. Well, there was music, enthusiastic singing, and an incredible welcome! I'd never experienced anything like it. It opened my eyes and sent me on a mission to experience and learn about all the different types of churches and religions I could find. That led me to explore and study other beliefs and started my search for spirit in all forms.

Take every opportunity to see life with fresh eyes and it opens up possibilities you wouldn't even consider when stuck in your old view.

If you're committed to growth and change you also can't always heed the overused refrain that says you should walk away if something isn't completely comfortable. This doesn't necessarily apply if you're seeking truth. Now, I'm all for listening to your gut, but you might consider that you're really disturbed because something new has been introduced into your reality threatening an outmoded paradigm.

It's your job to get to know yourself well enough to recognize if you're fleeing from a new expansive truth or experiencing a genuine threat to your existence. The more flexible you are in your life the easier this process becomes. If you're already too shut down, fearful, and resistant to any change, you'll reject the new information and make yourself unconscious to it to remain safe.

That's akin to fainting at the first sight of truth. It's always an option I suppose!

When in Doubt, Ask, "Is This Expansion or Contraction?"

o you feel light, free, happy, and enthused or fearful, defensive, angry, and closed off?

Don't you love being around people who are excited about life? The ones who take you on an unexpected excursion to buy plants for the garden and it becomes a grand adventure. Or the friend who sends you an e-mail about a new discovery in Egypt or posts a picture of the rainbow from the afternoon's shower. Expansion is fun to be around and feel. Qualities of an expansive nature are laughter, openness, enthusiasm, joy, and acceptance. You feel relief just being around them.

Contraction is most often a reaction to pain and fear. A drawing back of the soul to protect and defend its threatened turf. When contracted, you're defensive, negative, and resistant to anything new and often to the people around you. Your vision gets small and the world looks as big as the problem you're stuck on. It also can cause pain and illness as contraction tenses up the body, stressing all your physical systems.

Next time you're wavering on whether or not to try something new, ask yourself, "Does this cause me to expand or contract?" If it's the former, then take a deep breath and take the plunge.

Breath in ... breath out ... expand!

You Can Witness the Sacred and the Profane Driving Down the Highway

The dichotomy of human nature is not only present everywhere we go but within us. We can be tremendously kind and very selfish. We're here to experience these opposites and hopefully evolve to a less dramatic swing of emotions and actions.

The Buddha called this finding the middle way or the path of moderation and wisdom. For the Lakota Sioux, it's called Chanku Luta or a spiritual path to enlightenment and wisdom. Each culture has its own version of the journey to universal truth and the lessons needed to gain spiritual consciousness. All paths contain all things. So, with eyes open, you can observe the sacred (connection with God and reverence for all life) and the profane (irreverence and contempt for spirit) in your daily activities.

While driving down the highway on a boiling-hot summer day, tempers were short and I witnessed countless acts of anger and reckless driving as traffic backed up. Fingers were a-flying! There was very little regard for the safety of others and I felt in danger as I avoided yet another near-collision. I flashed on a story a friend told me the week before about driving home.

She came upon a hit-and-run accident where a young woman had been thrown from her car and was lying on the shoulder of the road. Running to her side, she knelt down in the mud beside her. There wasn't much she could offer besides holding her hand and telling her she wasn't alone and help was on the way. She heard the sounds of approaching sirens in the background as she gave her a healing and told her she was loved and would be all right. The paramedics arrived and quickly transported her to the hospital.

The woman survived the crash and after months of recovery looked up my friend to thank her and share she'd been certain she was going to die that night. But then an angel arrived who took her hand and told her she would be OK and she believed her. It was a simple miracle on the roadside.

Amidst disaster, anger, and impatience are opportunities to act with great compassion and kindness. They happen every day and we always have the option of deciding which side of this dichotomy we want to entertain.

For the rest of the day I drove slower and with greater respect for those on the road with me.

It's Better to Greet and Dance with Your Dark Side Than Deny It Exists

I'm a bit leery of people who're nice all the time or couples who say they never fight. Some of the greatest damage I ever received was at the hands of a so-called "nice" person. We're here to experience the range of emotion and unless you're a saint or a Buddha, you're going to feel and express it all daily.

There seems to be a lot of guilt and fear in even admitting to feelings we deem "bad." Learning to get along in a civilized way is about tempering the feelings of anger, fear, jealousy, competition, and sadness with enough self-awareness to ask why we're having them. The disconnect from our spiritual selves is what lets darker impulses take hold and causes us to lash out in unacceptable and destructive ways.

If you can't accept one side of yourself (the shadow) you won't feel the other side either (the light that comes from joy, love, and enthusiasm). If you don't own both and don't want to feel, even fun emotions can seem like a threat and be dismissed as out of control and immature. It's just too much feeling for them. Whoops! Did I just describe what many interpret as being an adult?

We temper the extreme swings in the dichotomies of dark and light as we learn to get along with each other in a world that requires conformity. But instead of owning these sides, we're encouraged to smother them and deny that those parts of us even exist. We develop social maturity but not necessarily spiritual maturity. Spiritual maturity is the free will to own both sides without judgement and in the light of truth choose where we want to stand.

Hopefully as we grow up, we learn to accept the polarity of dark and light within us and in the world. Denial of your darker emotions and impulses can cause them to erupt in a volcano of inappropriate reactions when sparked by a person or event. This really reinforces the self-judgement about "bad" emotions and damages relationships. Whether it's due to religious upbringing, societal pressure, or family programming, if you refuse to acknowledge the shadow side it'll bite you on the butt eventually.

Acknowledge those things you're afraid of about yourself, learn to understand them, and gain the self-trust that follows from loving the whole package. You can't really let go and experience joy if you're running from hidden feelings.

We all have a shadow side to own and learn from, so know that you're not alone in this. But developing a sense of humor about it takes away the power and allows you to *pas de deux*, blending your light into the darkness.

Darkness is simply the absence of light.

For humor: When caught up in, or avoiding your darker emotions; make up an absurd story about how horrendously bad or perfectly angelic you are. The more extreme it gets the funnier it will seem. Hopefully, some laughter will lead you back to a more balanced perspective!

Creativity

When a Creation is From Spirit There's Joy and Flow ... Not Effort

No effort doesn't mean you don't physically or mentally exert yourself to make something come true. It means the doing feels effortless because it flows from the creativity of your spirit. When your soul is being expressed through your creation, it becomes a drive. You don't care what people think, what time it is, or if you're getting paid for it.

When you're trying to will something to happen (third chakra) or in some way force a creation into existence, the result will usually not please you. You feel drained instead of energized by the act. It all depends on the source of the creation, not the physical steps that are taken to accomplish it.

If inspiration hits you, pursue it in any way you can. There are many brilliant, talented people who have great vision but lack the self-confidence or support to express it. The only difference between a successful self-expression and a failed one is actually doing it! Go ahead with your vision, no matter how out-there or unusual it may seem to you. Great art and invention has always come from one person whose fire to reveal their inner vision drove them to manifest it in the world.

What's one activity that engages your soul and lets time slip away? The days are going by anyway, you may as well leave something of yourself for all to see that says, "I was here!"

Taking it All Too Seriously?
Do Something Ridiculous!

I'm taken aback by how grim people look at times, driving next to me on the road or shopping in a store. I smile at them and it's as if they've forgotten how to acknowledge or return it. I know we can all feel overstressed occasionally, but not enough time to smile?

We're overloaded by the glut of information instructing us to exercise daily or eat a pristine, organic, gluten-, sugar-, and fat-free diet so we don't develop a host of terrifying maladies. By the way, did you do your brain exercises and learn something new today? Oh, yes, and what are you doing for your spiritual growth? Did you squeeze in that much-needed meditation or yoga class so you can ascend, transcend, and generally be enlightened?

Sigh ... is it any wonder we're overwhelmed by the should and should-nots we heed in order to thrive? Does this feel free to you; does it elicit joy and a light spirit? What does? Is there anything you do that's not for improvement but just for play? Are you so worried about how you appear to others you can't break the rules and do something truly outrageous for the fun of it?

Once I was distracted with worry over a project and needed to run to the post office for some supplies. At the counter, I looked down and noticed I had on two different shoes! The woman behind me and I started to laugh and I said, "Well, I had to do that as I have two left feet and I couldn't find a pair of shoes to fit."

A belly laugh shakes loose the cobwebs in the soul like nothing else. That ridiculousness was by accident, but it reminded me to not take myself so seriously or worry too much about what others think.

Spontaneity is in short supply these days but it's an earmark of amusement. So throw out the rules and duties and do something unexpected.

Dance like a maniac to your favorite song, give an absurd name when you order coffee, skip down the sidewalk and hope someone thinks you're crazy. Take paint and fling it on a canvas to see what happens. And for God's sake, smile at people!

Sometimes You Have to be Your Own Catalyst

What triggers growth in your life? Getting fired might be the catalyst needed to seek a new career. A divorce can become the impetus for increased self-awareness and the discovery of who you are and what you want in your life. An illness often leads to searching for new ways of caring for yourself and consequently better health. Dramatic life events can be the catalyst needed to guide us to new paths and growth. Even positive recognition about success for an accomplishment can inspire us with more confidence to take on new challenges.

All life events can teach us who we are by observing our reaction to them, and you can get to know yourself by paying attention to your responses to those dramatic catalysts. This generates the awareness you need to choose a step instead of waiting for external stimulus to jumpstart your creativity. Creating from necessity is creating with survival as the catalyst. The juice runs out when the survival is quenched. This winds up feeling like treading water to stay afloat, never getting to the destination.

But what if there are no external factors kick-starting growth? How about the regular mundane weeks and days where life goes along and there's no influence to direct you to a new step? Talking (and listening) to yourself in those quiet times of your life can help you discover your true path. Listening to your spiritual muse is much easier when it's not trying to shout down external voices and events demanding your immediate attention

We're here to express the brilliance of our spirit through this body we created for that purpose. The spark of our deepest soul generates the enthusiasm and joy necessary to go from thought to manifestation in your life. If a creation is birthed by spirit, that connection is nourished and you'll persevere through any obstacle you encounter.

Take the time to hear what your inner voice is telling you. It's as important to check in with yourself during times of relative calm as it is when you are frantically putting out fires. If there was nothing you had to do today, what would you want to do?

Creative Drift and Aimless Floating Can Inspire!

*W*e live in complicated, busy times with too much of our energy and time used up by the simple act of living. When do we have the space to actually find our creative dream and put it into action? Quick, you better read a book or listen to a podcast about it!

As a child, I recall hours of time spent wandering near a creek by my house or lying in the grass, staring at the sky and picturing things I would like to do in my life. I believe it's called imagination. Ideally as children, we're removed enough from care and worry to have those peaceful moments to let our fantasies fly.

As adults, we're so over-scheduled and distracted that we don't make time and space for sitting and staring at the clouds or just having *fun*—allowing the bubbling up of joy that inspires creativity. Perhaps that's why we tend to judge spontaneous people as acting childish.

Adult relaxation takes the form now of sports, yoga, meditation, prayer, recreational substances, or some other sort of improvement activity. But you are still "doing" something. However, to simply float and let yourself drift where the spirit wants to go can be unnerving. It requires letting go of structure, duty, and self-improvement and just being who you are. Guilt and responsibility be gone!

There's an outdoor art garden I like to meander in when I need to stoke the fire. I wander along the path admiring the wild, imaginative expression of the artists' vision. They change the installations frequently and like life, you never know what you'll find as you round the bend in the road. Other times I sit and watch the ocean waves for hours with no intent at all—just enjoying the breeze and the movement of the water.

Many people take vacations to get away from responsibility and find that creative drift to refresh the inner voice. But if you don't already do this regularly, the expectation on the vacation to set things right can make for a disappointing time. If it does work, but your schedule gives you no space, you may dread your return to normal life.

I highly recommend frequent drifting. Find an afternoon with nothing to do and go where you feel like a kid; gaze at the vast sky, ponder the power of the ocean, or climb a hill or mountain and marvel at the world at your feet. Let your wildest dreams come to the surface and dance through your mind. Later, notice what stays with you; that's your vision. It's tremendously satisfying to actively follow where that inspiration leads. Let the muse take you!

Breathe deeply the fresh air of the moment and breathe out all the expectation, responsibility, and worry from your body. Stretch your arms up over your head to the sun and then reach down and touch the ground. Feel your connection to this beautiful earth. Look around; see what you see and hear what's within you. Drift with that for a while.

Be Open to the Unexpected and the Impossible– It Makes Life Amazing ... or at Least Interesting

*R*ules are the name of the game and they're shoved at us constantly to dictate how things are supposed to happen in life. We're programmed to believe there are mandatory steps to follow to obtain certain results or achieve success. Some of these are valuable. Should you decide to run a marathon, it may be wise to train in increments and build up your distance so you don't collapse with a medical emergency. However, spiritual growth does not travel in a logical straight line; B does not necessarily follow A in the world of spirit. We can get stuck on the rules of the body and mind and lose our ability to receive a miracle. Spirit transcends the rules.

I've witnessed hopeless medical cases completely healed by the patients' unexpected spiritual awakening. A chance meeting with an inaccessible publisher in a bar led to a friend's book being published! Allowing these miracles to occur has a lot to do with your ability to relinquish control and expectation. Amazing opportunities being presented to you can be passed by when you don't let go and let it happen.

I see this same issue when counseling those who complain they can't find a good relationship. Holding on to unrealistic pictures and expectations about the perfect partner, they reject the gift of the wonderful person who just offered to buy them coffee.

Too many rules, fears, and duties can cut us off from the thread of spirit that connects us and delivers those unexpected detours to fulfill our dreams. Gifts manifest in unforeseen adventures when you trust your inner voice and go with the flow you've stepped into. The more you do this the more miracles occur. Since your spirit draws this stuff to you when you ask for it, say yes when you get what you want. Don't think the miracle to death!

There's the opportunity for wonder all around us and support when you least expect it. Keep your eyes open to the infinite possibilities that happen in even a casual conversation. God does indeed work in mysterious ways. You'll never be bored if you let the unexpected and amazing visit you.

Remember, All of This
May Not be True

As we grow older, ideally, we amend what we think to be true when we receive new information. However, learning new things gets a lot more difficult the longer we're set in a belief system. We become way too comfortable traversing the well-worn pathways to our habits and patterns, filling our lives with people who agree with and reinforce it.

Occasionally, just possibly, for an ever-so-short moment, consider that what you hold to be true is in fact not.

Your view of yourself is a good start. Are you holding on to an old concept someone gave you about who you are? Could it be you no longer have to live up or down to that image? Maybe you actually are good at (or at least enjoy) math, art, sports, music, dancing, computers, or whatever someone else said you couldn't do.

It could be as simple as challenging your personal likes and dislikes or as big as adapting your world view. Start by examining your true thoughts and emotions about a situation as opposed to going along with what you or others think you're supposed to feel. You might even discover you really like and admire a person you previously judged, get to enjoy a new cuisine, or find truth in a new philosophy.

The paradigms of this world are shifting rapidly and your truth may have to be fluid rather than fixed to adapt and thrive. This was echoed to me in the answer a friend gave when I recently asked why he loves surfing so much and what it taught him. His wise words seemed a perfect analogy for succeeding in the midst of change.

"I get to experience exhilaration and failure on the same wave and the patience of waiting. I 've had to let go of what I can't control and realize that some things are far bigger than me. I've learned to be humble, pay attention, stay in the moment, think, have respect, and not take anything for granted. Each wave is unique and I never know what's going to happen, but If I relax and stay open, I can always find my balance. Mostly, I've learned that just when I think I know it all, I really don't know anything. Oh, yes ... and did I mention to try and try again?"

Might be time for all of us to go surfing!

The things that challenge our truth and put us in a giant brain press happen when asked to stretch your view and see things differently—expanding your mind, so to speak. You can rise to the occasion and open up to new vision or close up and justify your unchanging position. We're always being offered the opportunity to look at life on a bigger screen and explore a new universe. So stay present and don't get too comfortable with your view; tomorrow you may find it's too small.

Remember, you don't have to believe anything I've said either.

Energy Basics

The Seven Body Chakras

*T*he word chakra comes from Sanskrit and means spinning wheel or circle, which is how they appear to those who can see energy. There are many other chakras both in and out of the body.

The main chakras are energy centers located along the middle of the spiritual or energy body and in the palms of your hands and feet. Ideally they're connected with lines of energy flowing between them (channels) communicating what you need for a balanced life. They're more open or closed depending on the life lessons you're experiencing, damage incurred, or the energy response called for at any given time. An all-open or all-closed chakra can cause an imbalance or lack of energy but can tell you where you need some growth. They can be consciously healed and opened or closed at will.

1. **First** (root): This is the center for well-being and manifestation in the physical world. This chakra holds the information you need to take care of and maintain your physical self. It lets you know when you're in danger and sends signals for action

needed to survive. When grounded, it makes you feel more at home and safe in your body. If ungrounded and too open, it triggers a stress response, generating an exaggerated fight-or-flight reaction over minor issues. This can send excessive energy through the body causing an abundance of physical and emotional problems (as in post-traumatic stress disorder). Color: **Red**

2. **Second** (sacral): This is where we find the freedom to have and learn from all the emotions and enjoyment of the sensual/ sexual energies of the body. When sensitive to others' feelings and realities, a healthy second chakra radiates empathy. It's the center that registers emotions (yours and others) and the sensual enjoyment of the world. In balance, you experience passion in life and intimacy with others as well as connection both emotionally and physically. If overused and wide open, it makes you too emotional, insecure, sexual, and reactive. Blocked, it can cause addiction to the sensations of the physical world in order to feel (sex, substance abuse, adrenaline rush, power, money, pain) or create coldness and a lack of sensitivity. Some physical symptoms of imbalance are: lower back pain, urinary tract and kidney infections, reproductive problems, and intestinal upset. Color: **Orange**

3. **Third** (solar plexus): Here we develop the ability to take action, express personal power, and relate to the rest of the world. Will, control, action, confidence, and balance are some of the gifts of the third chakra. If wide open, out of alignment, or blocked we can become fearful and insecure or too controlling, aggressive, and/or dominant. It's also one of the doorways we use for astral (out of the body) travel. If emotional or controlling energy is being tossed your way you will most often feel it here.

Stomach, adrenal, fatigue, and digestive issues are common when this chakra is blocked or damaged. Color: **Yellow**

4. **Fourth** (heart): The center of affinity, or the ability to love yourself and others, resides here. The upper chakras (spiritual) and the lower chakras (physical) come together in the body to connect to others with compassion and understanding. A healthy fourth chakra fills you with the peaceful sense of oneness and connection to all things. When closed or unhealthy, you may get withdrawn, lonely, depressed, and insensitive to the emotions of other people and animals. If too open or unbalanced, it can lead to neediness and dependence on others to fill you with love and can cause you to seek external validation. There may be heart, lung, and mid-back problems if blocked. Color: **Green**

5. **Fifth** (throat): The fifth chakra controls how you express your soul to the world through communication and what you create. If open, balanced, and clear we speak our truth freely and are willing to listen to others without judgement. It's also where soul inspiration is filtered to the other chakras so you can take action and bring dreams into fruition in the physical realm. If closed and unbalanced, you may "bite your tongue," holding back your words and thoughts, and be quiet, shy, and unassertive. At times, this stops your creations from manifesting due to a lack of energy or confidence. When unbalanced, it also can manifest as manipulation of others using words to get what you want or as weapons (insults, gossip) to injure. Neck, throat, thyroid, and dental issues are common physical symptoms of fifth chakra issues. Color: **Blue**

6. **Sixth** (brow): It's called the third eye because when open, it allows you to see beyond the physical and "read" emotions,

energy, images, and spiritual beings around you. The attributes of a healthy third eye are intuition, discernment, neutrality, and seeing the truth in all things. When open and balanced you get the eyes of spiritual wisdom and connection to the higher planes of awareness. When turned off or out of balance, it can lead to obsessive thinking, confusion, helplessness, and perceiving the world through emotions and images of the past experiences and beliefs you're stuck in. If you can't see the truth for yourself, it can make you an easy person to control or program. Headaches, vision and sinus issues, and cloudy thinking may occur with problems here. The pineal gland is closely linked to the ability of clairvoyance. Color: **Indigo**

7. **Seventh** (crown): Located on the top of the head, this is your direct connection to higher spiritual power and truth (God, the Universe, etc.). When open and connected to the spiritual realm you are certain, peaceful, powerful, and able to receive truth easily with no ego involvement. It's the source of harmony felt in the alignment of body and spirit. If disconnected or damaged, there's a sense of loneliness and isolation. With no spiritual connection, you experience feelings of despair, powerlessness, confusion, lack of self-trust, and loss of purpose in your life. Symptoms of outside influence in the crown leads to blindly following anyone perceived as stronger or more knowledgeable and seeking information outside yourself. Color: **Violet**

Many of the definitions you'll see in the prolific rainbow chakra charts assign a particular color symbolizing optimum health. However, there's usually a variety of colors (vibrations of energy) present in each chakra; it shifts depending on the lesson you are working on at the time and what energy you're holding in it. Don't get stuck on trying to make it a certain color. It's more relevant to observe what the dominant energy is, ask why it's present, determine if it's yours, and see what the lesson is. If you don't like what's there, you can always ask for what you want to change it to and fill it with that vibration (color).

Hand chakras are located in the palms of the hand. They open and close as the flow of healing and creative energy runs through your energy channels in the arms. Energy can be consciously directed through them from any of the other chakras for healing ourselves and others and into creative projects. They also act as receivers to read information from the energy of others and transmit it back to the other chakras. We often have one hand that's stronger as a receiver and one that's stronger as a sender of info and energy. Healers often have hot hands. There are also chakras in the shoulder, elbow, wrist, and fingers.

Feet chakras are found in the arches and sole of the foot. They open to the flow of energy from the earth, drawing it up leg channels into the chakras, and help you feel connected to nature and the spirit of the earth. They act as another grounding spot to release unwanted energy from your body. That's why it feels so good to take off your shoes and walk in the grass or sand. Many significant pressure points here contribute to the healthy flow of energy throughout the body. You can also ground from the outsides of the feet (taught in many of the martial arts). There's a reason a healthy person is said to have both feet planted firmly on the ground!

There are many other minor chakras in the body (all joints have them) as well as five more above your head. For now, it's challenging enough to just become aware of and heal the ones listed here. Walk first; run later.

Grounding

*I*f you tell someone to get grounded they almost always know what you're talking about. We even have common sayings reflecting this like, "She's got her feet planted firmly on the ground" or "His approach is grounded in reality." Even electrical systems are grounded for safety.

Grounding helps you, the spirit, be connected to the body and the earth you walk upon. When ungrounded you feel spacey, confused, not present, and indecisive. The lights are on and nobody's home. Making a spiritual connection to the body and the earth keeps your spirit present in the body and conscious of the world around you. Consequently, you are much safer and more alert to the choices you need to make for daily well-being. Some of the activities people do to feel grounded are exercising, gardening, eating (particularly heavy foods like pasta and meat), and anything that makes the body feel safe. Even a warm bath can help.

There are many variations to grounding. Any intent to connect your spirit to your body and the earth will anchor you. Visualize a connection (tree trunk, waterfall, light beam, etc.) from the base of the spine (or first chakra) down into the planet and let gravity help you be more present. Grounding the edges of the aura, from the feet and from other chakras, is also useful.

Re-owning Your Energy

When you give away too much of your life force, it leaves you feeling depleted. You may be losing your energy to problems, people, or activities in your daily life and need to reclaim some of your good stuff to re-energize yourself. It's as simple as taking a moment to call back your energy from where you've left it in your world and focus it back within yourself.

Intent is a powerful thing and the mere act of consciously intending something makes it real. Be in this moment and imagine energy flowing back to you like little rivers of light filling a reservoir above your head. When it seems full, pull the plug, releasing the energy to wash down, around, and through you as if standing under a waterfall. As you fill up, stretch, take a couple deep breaths, and enjoy how it revitalizes every cell of your body.

Bonus for Readers of Enlighten-Up!

Get a FREE audio download from Cathy Langlois featuring simple techniques to help you find your balance, regain focus, increase your enthusiasm for the world around you, and live a more centered life. The audio includes three parts:

Grounding & Releasing: You'll feel more present by connecting your spirit and body to the earth. You can then easily let go of problems that block your natural flow of energy and restore a sense of peace.

Re-owning Life Force: (Chi) This is a powerful but simple way to replenish your life force and call back all the energy you've been giving away (problems, people, projects etc.).

Protection: A visualization to help you create a safety zone from negative people and events.

Download your FREE audio at
www.SpiritHorseCenter.com/bonus

About the Author

At four years old, I freaked out my parents by waking them in the middle of the night to ask, "Can we talk about infinity?" I alarmed the neighbors by announcing unknown pregnancies and even worse that the father was not the husband! I stopped giving messages to people from those who had passed on when I saw the fear and anger in their eyes instead of the happiness I thought it would bring. I soon learned that keeping my awareness to myself might ensure I actually made it to adulthood. I was aware at a very young age that though I was in a child's body, I'd lived many lifetimes before. I've always had extra sensitive abilities and have spent considerable time and commitment developing and learning to control them.

Miraculously, I emerged from a dark and stormy childhood without winding up in a rehab clinic. Though I admit that in my frenzy to escape pain and experience the world I tried everything. I survived Catholic school, drugs, sex, rock and roll, hitchhiking cross-country, anti-war demonstrations, college, a couple cults, heartbreak, betrayal, being an ordained minister, therapy, horse ownership, spiritual pilgrimages to many countries, and a career in radio and television.

Each experience was valuable and contributed to my ability to not only survive, but thrive.

Seeking insight about what was going on in my life, I read any book I could get my hands on. I put myself through college, taking any class that interested me (must be why it took so long) regardless of how it contributed to a degree. Upon graduating, I realized traditional learning wasn't enough anymore. I yearned for deeper answers and eventually found myself diving into the world of spiritual teachings, practices, and wisdom traditions. Ultimately, I discovered the great secret; surprise...your answers are within you.

This path led me to leave the Midwest and a job in television to travel the country, where I stumbled into some amazing adventures. I learned to talk (and listen) to plants from an herbalist in Oregon. A Native American man from the Black Hills of South Dakota taught me to make fire in the rain and read the past in the smoke. I accidentally ran into and had my journey blessed by the Dalai Lama in Colorado (I had no idea who he was at the time, but he seemed nice). Eventually I landed in Northern California.

Enthusiastic for more knowledge, I discovered an organization offering spiritual training for sensitive, psychic people. Studying there for many years, I eventually became a branch director and teacher. As paths will do, at some point mine diverged from theirs and it was time to move on. This led me to open my own spiritual training center in 1991. I believe you can find truth everywhere, so I continued on to learn from a myriad of different approaches to spiritual development and healing. I borrow freely from all of them as needed to assist in finding answers and clarity.

Called to further explore the great mysteries, I flew with the condor's spirit in Machu Picchu, stood in the middle of inexplicable crop circles in England, received miraculous psychic surgery in the Philippines, picked chamomile in an ancient healing center in Greece, meditated in the Great Pyramid of Giza, shared prayer with the Whirling Dervishes in Turkey, got dizzy in the vortexes of Sedona, and gazed into the center of an ancient crystal skull.

For thirty-six years, I've given thousands of spiritual readings, healings, and classes using the knowledge I've gained on developing our natural abilities to explore the mystery and wonder of the spiritual realm. I've never stopped learning and believe we're all teachers to each other no matter the role. I'm devoted to seeking truth even when it's painful for me to face it.

These are some personal truths I've learned on my journey. I hope they stimulate you to question and explore your own part here on this planet.

Cathy Langlois is director/owner of The Spirit Horse Center in Northern California. She shares a cozy home with the funniest, most compassionate, and wisest of men, her husband (Bob), and six rescued critters.

www.SpiritHorseCenter.com
Cathy@SpiritHorseCenter.com